After I Pulled the

Trigger:

Surviving Suicide's Lie

by Clinging to Hope's

Truth

James L. Atkisson

Other titles:
"When Angel Intervenes"
"Big Valley Football: The Legend of the Badgers"
by Christian Price

"A Change of Heart: From Suicide to Life"
By: James L. Atkisson

www.fromsuicidetolife.com

Dedicated to those of us that pulled the trigger and wished we could have the moment just before over again.
May your voice join mine.

The Thief comes only to steal and to kill and to destroy
I have come that they may have life and have it to the full
John 10:10

Cover design by: Darleen Dixon

WHEN AN ANGEL INTERVENES

One of my favorite stories in the bible is found in the book of John Chapter 9. It's the story of the "blind beggar." This man has gone to the village square for his daily meal. He spends his days living in the dust chasing after scraps tossed out from a passerby. I'm sure his life's value at the time was no greater than the livestock bought and sold in the market place. His life and affliction are discussed openly as if he's on public display. Little did this man know his life was about to be changed. He was about to feel a touch and it would be a touch forever changing his life. The man went from a blind beggar to a man who could see. An outcast, blind broken man's life recorded and remembered for thousands of years. This man's life is only remembered because of the one who touched him and the life transforming power of the touch.

I'm sure this man was overwhelmed by what happened to his life. He felt compelled to share with his neighbors the good news: he'd been given sight. Did the neighbors embrace and rejoice with him? Picking up at verse 8 in the New International Version Bible, history recorded what happened to him: They hurl insults, question his identity, make demands of him and drag him before the council where he must give an account of his claims. There will be no celebrating, no inclusive feelings and no well wishes towards him. In the face of a hostile crowd he doesn't falter and holds fast to his testimony. The man is insulted and cast out from among them. In verse 35 Jesus hears the man has been thrown out and goes to find the man. The man knows the voice and who is speaking with him and bows before the one whom transformed his life. There's no value to this story without first knowing what the condition of his life was like before his famous encounter. In verse 25, the man best sums up his testimony with one sentence: *"I was blind but now I see."*

I believe I can find similarities between my life and this man's life. Our lives were radically altered by a touch. His life's story wouldn't be complete if the story didn't mention what his life was like before the touch. My life's story would not be complete if I didn't say what my life was transformed from. The beggar met resistance when he shared his life's story; likewise, I met sharp resistance when I've tried to share what the transforming power did to my life. His life was put on display in the market. My life has been the subject of whispered conversations. It's also been taunted, snickered, belittled, mocked and held in contempt. I was told to lie about my own life and never share what I'd been delivered from. The man, when he met the one whom changed his life, bowed his knee. I also owe my life to the one that saved and transformed my life.

This is my second attempt at telling my story and my second book. My first book was titled "When an Angel Intervenes" and it began as a short story to enter a local writing contest. I wrote "When an Angel Intervenes" based on the suggestion of my wife. My wife knew my life's story, what I'd been saved from, and she wanted me to share it with others. She wanted me to share one page from my life's story. The page she wanted me to write about occurred on January 24, 1986 at approximately 4:45 in the evening. The reason why this moment was so important to my wife and she thought I should write it down because this was the moment I'd chosen to set myself free of life's depression through suicide. The plan I'd drawn up had me go into an isolated wooden area away from help with a rifle. I placed the rifle over my heart and pulled the trigger. The moment was over faster than a blink of an eye but its consequences have lasted for decades. I believe each day following that moment have been a gift to me. I wish I could confess I've lived my life in accordance with this understanding and I treasured each passing moment but it'd be insincere if I tried to paint that picture.

When I sat down to write my story, I struggled with how to put it together because of the two decades of fear, misunderstanding and shame surrounding what I'd done to myself. With a bit of creative effort two characters were born: *"Bill"* and *"Billy."* I placed Bill at the beginning of the story busy with life as he prepares to attend his twenty year high school reunion with his wife Erika. Bill is struggling to keep a lid on things as he feels the stress and strain of life press in on him from all sides. The couple starts out for what should be an enjoyable evening, but as the couple gets closer to their destination Bill's heart is troubled by echoes from his past. Their destination is Bill's old high school and it serves as a sonar beacon. With each sonic ping, the dread of facing his past mounts. Bill tries to redirect the couple's original plan as he throws out alternative ideas for the evening but to no avail and Bill reluctantly arrives at the school. Bill and Erika find a place to park and as they walk through fog on a dark winter's night, peering at them is their destination but it resembles a haunted house and not a school. Bill senses glaring eyes of his past peering at him through the murky night as they approach the door to the school.

Bill and Erica enter the school and Bill's concerns are realized as a ghost- like fog burns away to reveal a never ending- loop of history. Bill is forced to relive certain aspects of his childhood when the fog burns away to reveal Billy standing in a hallway looking at him. My life's experiences gave life to Bill as he watches his younger counterpart take a walk into secluded woods. On more than one occasion, I've had to watch myself take a similar walk. In those final moments Billy offers up a prayer asking to be delivered from this moment.

Some days this moment is very fresh in my mind. A frosty breeze on a cold January evening and it doesn't matter where I'm at or what I'm doing. It's there before me to relive once again. Along with my suicide note and rifle, I took a bible with me. The bible was grabbed in haste and I hoped it would bring words of peace to my broken heart.

I lived in a rural area at the time and there were more woods and empty fields than homes. The acres of wooded lands were used for hunting and recreational shooting. It was an ideal place for recreational shooting and target practice. It wasn't out of place to hear random gunfire from time to time. I chose a wooded plot of land behind my home because it was secluded and peaceful. I walked a little over a quarter of a mile and stopped walking when I reached a small creek. Next to this creek I found a small crate. It made an ideal resting stool for me to sit and work up the nerve to see my purpose through. I never tasted a drop of alcohol at this point in my life and I didn't know what an illegal drug was so my mind was free from chemicals.

The struggle to load the rifle and pull the trigger went on for forty- five minutes. At the end of this struggle

I'd drifted off to sleep from exhaustion. What this nap did was clear my mind and I realized I couldn't follow through with it. *I wasn't able to shoot myself.* I felt as if I was locked in a deadly game of chicken and at the last minute I blinked and the will to live won over at the last possible moment. I stood up and had every intention of walking out of the woods and returning the rifle where I'd found it.

What made me freeze in mid stride and reconsider, I was facing some dreadful consequences in the coming days and was very afraid to face them so I turned and walked back to the crate. Like an exhausted swimmer, I sank below the surface for what I'd thought was going to be the last time. It was time to bring this plan to a close. I'd closed my eyes and asked God to *"send an Angel to save me from this moment."*

After saying amen Billy opens his eyes and feels despair at the sight of an empty woodland. Accepting the time has come; Billy opens the action, loads the gun, closes the action and removes the safety. He slides his hand down the rifle while looking up into the sky for a focal point. He pauses for a moment and then depresses the trigger.

The weight of disappointment was adding to my sense of isolation. I truly believed prior to my prayer God was going to speak directly to me. A thought was introduced to me and it centered around: *"God doesn't care because he's too busy."* I was overwhelmed with stress and it felt like the trees were alive and huddled around me doing their best to taunt me. From somewhere deep in the woods, it sounded like voices were chanting in unison. Instead of chanting for me to **"Jump!"** the cries I heard were **"Shoot!"** There wasn't a bird, chipmunk or squirrel to be seen or heard. Other than the gentle sounds from the creek and the whispers in my ears the woods were very still.

Though it was Billy depressing the trigger from the past It's Bill that recoils in the present day as once more the sensation of red hot steel is blasted into his thin body. As Bill holds onto his wife she unknowingly has become her husband's lifeline to the present. Erika is unaware of the savage and ferocious memory that just kidnapped her husband's mind and body. Erika feels her husband's body tense for a brief moment and thinks nothing of it as Bill feels the full effects of what's been unleashed into his life.

It was a .22 caliber rifle and it was loaded with a hollow point bullet. I chose this small rifle because it was easier to conceal as I left my home that day. One reason why I survived was my reluctance to pay attention in anatomy class. I was thinking of oath taking ceremonies and where the oath taker places his hand so I aimed an inch from my hearts true position. The first thing I remember coming from the end of the barrel was a brilliant flash of light because light always moves faster than sound. The sound of the rifle startled me because it was a small caliber in relation to larger caliber rifles. I wasn't prepared for how loud it sounded but I'd never been on the end of a gun before when it went off either. The blast from the rifle seemed like it went on for an eternity as it slowly meandered its way through the woods. It felt as if a professional baseball player picked up a hickory bat and swung against my chest with the intent of sending one out of the park. The moment was over in a flash but twenty six years later the actual bullet scar remains tender to the touch.

While lying on the ground Billy begins to feel a sense of remorse for what he's done. He tries to not think about it because it's too late for that. Once a bullet leaves the barrel the moment is gone forever.

While lying on the ground I took a few gasps and was shocked I was still alive. The kinetic energy was dreadful, and it drove me to my feet. I stumbled around for a brief moment until my legs gave out and I collapsed to the ground in a withered heap. I'd prayed to God before I'd depressed the trigger and it was His name on my lips when I landed on the ground. I laid in shock for a period of time and didn't move until the ringing in my ears was gone and I could see through the camera flash in front of my eyes. I could taste gunpowder. It was bitter with a hint of brass I assume from the bullet casing. Once my senses were in order, I glanced down towards my feet and was surprised to see only a small tear in the fabric of the coat. The rip was deceiving because for a brief moment I'd felt a sense of optimism. I naively believed I'd be able to climb to my feet and shake off what I'd done because the tear was only the size of a pencil eraser. The optimism was quickly replaced with dread when my clothes became soaked with what felt like warm creamy soup and my nose was filled with a hot sticky aroma. I was bleeding heavily, and I could feel it running all over me. I started to have a strong sense of regret at this point. I tried to push it aside because I didn't want my final moments filled with this regret. It was more important to prepare myself to accept the consequences for pulling the trigger but something happened next that meant the difference between life and death.

Billy hears an unfamiliar voice speak with him. He was alone in the woods just before pulling the trigger. Billy knows the sounds of his own thoughts but what enters his mind wasn't the sound of his minds voice. It gets his attention like a soft welcoming breeze on a stifling summer day. The voice offers a refuge from the gathering storm and it blunts the primitive fear trying to absorb his mind while his condition deteriorates. The voice doesn't say much to Billy and time was of critical importance but it presented a choice to Billy. It asked, "Name a reason to live." Billy could finish the journey he'd started months ago, a journey that led him to this place or look for a reason to hope for and altar his course to a new path. The new path could lead him towards life.

The woods were unforgivingly cold as the earth stole the warmth from my body. I was certain a fully developed adult male was standing on my sternum and driving me into the earth. There was something coming for me and I wasn't prepared to meet it. There was an overwhelming sense of not wanting to die alone in the woods. It was when this wave of fear started to break through the walls of my mind that **"IT"** spoke with me. It was a voice and a pulse of energy at the same time. In the same way water ripples through a still pond after a stone is cast into it, this pulse rippled through me. At one moment I was afraid of being alone until the voice calmed my fears. I sensed I was being held and though I couldn't see anyone around me. My voice doesn't have the authority or conviction in it to speak to the fear I was facing at that moment in time and calm the storm. The five words it said to me presented me with an option. Accept what suicide had led me to do or find a reason to hope for and leave this place and live my life.

Following the question from an unseen voice Billy tries to think of a reason to live for. What came to him weren't dreams and hopes typically discussed by his peers during lunch at school. What came to him were the sounds of children playing, laughing and living. There were powerful impressions and hopes deposited in his heart and mind. Precious moments a father may feel in life as he shares his life with his children. In the midst of the ugly and violent nature of the world he'd found himself apart of, there was a beautiful life going on around him from another time and place. Though the trees towered around him and were satisfied he'd pushed the trigger, he had the loving embrace of a family he'd never known before.

After the voice spoke to me the only thing I could think of was how much stress I was under. I felt like I was drowning and my legs were weak. I knew I wanted to answer whoever it who spoke to me. I'd rolled over into the fetal position and it was then the next pulse surged through me. I'd heard the sound of children around me. The moments deposited in my heart were many of the same tender moments I treasure today, and it was a promise made to me. There are times when my children are playing in a crowded room with many other children. The room is buzzing with life and though I can't see my children my mind locks onto their sounds and quickly sorts through the other sounds. My intuition knows the sound of my children and finds them quickly over the sounds of the other children's voices. When I'd heard the sound of life, it was powerful enough to draw me out of the curled up protective position and push me towards life.

Billy seems to live a full life in those critical moments. Even though he can't undo the damage done from the bullet, he can certainly try and get to help. He may not make it to help in time, but he decides it'd be better to die fighting for his life than just lying on the ground waiting to accept his fate.

I'd found a reason to live for. I'd been given hope and spoke out into the woods I wanted to live and knew in my heart I wanted to live a full life. In that critical moment in time one of my true heart's desires was revealed to me. The brief pulse of energy moving through me was powerful enough to reverse the tide carrying me to an end before I'd even had a chance to start my life.

The voice speaks again to Billy. It told him "That is a good reason, crawl now." Billy climbs to his feet and moves through the woods with the precision of a drunkard stumbling in the dark attempting to get out of the woods. With little or no warning, the ground falls away and he collapses to the ground with a solid crash feeling as though it's a futile effort to try and get to the safety of a phone so help could be summoned. Once more the voice calls out to him but this time with a more firm tone it said, "Crawl."

and Billy tries to crawl through the woods in an effort to get to help.

I remember using the tree I'd sat against to climb to my feet. I'd tried to run through the woods but it was more like a fast falling stumbling forward clutching motion grasping at whatever tree in arms reach as I passed by. I felt I couldn't trust my legs or feet anymore. With no warning the ground would shift sharply to the right of left, or it would jump forwards or fall back as if the ground became alive under my feet. I'd just collapse to the ground without the aid of my arms to break my fall. It wasn't possible to get out of the woods and sometimes it felt as if a tree would dart out in front of me to block my path. The burden of the man standing on my chest had been transferred to my back, and it was a struggle to move ten to fifteen yards at a time. It spoke to me again and this time it sounded like a parent speaking to a child in a stern controlled voice. It said **"CRAWL!"** My extremities had the strength of gelatin as I worked against the strain of dead weight on my back and shoulders. When I was at the crate I was using a tremendous amount of energy just trying to protect myself in a curled up position. Trying to work through the obstacle dense terrain was a different struggle of its own. From the moment I went to the ground for the last time there's no memory of clearing the woods. There was a faint sensation my body was bouncing off the ground with considerable force. When I woke up in the ICU, I asked why I couldn't open my left eye. They told me *"your eye is swollen shut from the damage you caused when you dragged yourself through the woods."* I barely had the strength to stand on my two feet. I believe I was aided in getting free from the cover of the woods. The woods were mainly clear of low hanging vegetation other than an occasional briar patch. The struggle was the erratic nature in which my vision distorted the distances between trees, rocks and stumps. My keeper was insistent I move to ground and stay down. It would've taken a considerable amount of time and energy covering the necessary distance on my stomach than upright and walking.

*Once Billy clears the woods and enters the field he hears the voice for the last time. It tells him **"Call for help."** Billy begins a battle for survival in the field. He does what the voice tells him to do and despite no one being in ear shot, Billy starts to cry out for help. While lying in the field he sees the damage he'd inflicted on himself.*

The last time he looked it'd only been a small tear in his jacket, but a second look told a much different story. He begins to sense the world changing around him. His perception of reality starts to shift in ways that are foreign to him. He feels as if he's falling into the sky and is afraid to look into the sky and decided to look at the trees because they provide a fixed reference point. With no reference points in the sky there's nothing there to tell him he hasn't gone onto the next life. Billy continues to cry for help until he hears footsteps approaching him.

I found myself in a field and no longer moving. Once more I felt the pulse of energy course through me and it wanted me to call out for help. This was the last time I ever heard it. Even though there was no one within ear shot, it still wanted me to call out. I thought the warm moist vapor rising from my breathing had as much chance of grabbing a person's attention as my weak voice had of breaking the barrier of an empty field. There was very little hope of anyone hearing me or seeing me. It felt like I was trying to yell under water and I'd made the mistake of looking down at my feet. I was upset that my shoes were gone and I'd walked into the woods with a fresh powder blue coat without a stain on it. I'd gotten it as a Christmas

Present one month prior. The coat was a blood soaked, tattered rag covered with mud, twigs, moss, and briars. I promised to never look back down there again.

It was while I was lying in the field my perception of reality started to shift. There was a very distinct sensation of something separating away from me. I felt my heart quiver and shake. There was the sense of falling into the sky while the ground fell away. The sky was a place to step into, and I didn't like this sensation. I focused on the trees and thought as long as I could see a tree then I was alive. I'm not sure how long I laid there but I'd come as far as I was going to get and they'd find my body in the field the next day. Up to that moment I felt like my cries had been nothing more than whimpers. The last one was more than a whimper because it took wings and soared up into the sky.

Billy hears the sound of rushing feet. He glances over his shoulder and sees his brother running towards him. Billy tells his brother what'd happen and his brother runs to get help. There was nothing else Billy could do but lay still and hope it wasn't too late for him. After a short period of time he hears more footsteps running and sees his grandfather running at him like the young fit man he'd been in the past. His grandfather had called for help and they were on their way. He'd have to rely on the volunteer system to respond from their places of employment, farms, or homes to their apparatus and drive the fifteen minutes to the field Billy was waiting in. Billy drifts away and loses track of time when his grandfather kneels by his side. He wouldn't realize his fear of dying alone in the woods. He wakes up to find the police around him wanting to know if he'd done this to himself while emergency staff members prepare to transport him to the hospital.

The voice offered choice and hope to me. When people are depressed and blind from personal pains they can become blind in their desire to be set free. For some, suicide seems to be the only choice to be free from the pain and hope is an almost unheard of commodity. It was hope that made me climb up off the ground and a choice that made my feet move to get help. The voice led me towards safety and though I couldn't hear or see anyone, it was working on my behalf in another reality. From where I was no one could've seen me from a casual glance. They'd have to come down looking for me because there were multiple obstructions blocking points of view. My brother was compelled to leave the warmth and comfort of the house and go stack firewood. It was an urgent compulsion and he should go *now.* I saw him running towards me and felt a tremendous sense of relief and joy. I knew I'd been instructed to yell for help. The last time I saw my brother he was relaxing on the couch watching one of his favorite television programs. By the time he found me I was wracked with painful bouts of shivering, unable to breathe, and in and out of consciousness. I knew as he ran off to get help it was more than my imagination I'd been interacting with. The presence told me to call out for help despite my thought; *this is hopeless no one will hear me but they did and it brought help to me.*

Billy's struggle to survive went on that day. His perception of reality would continue to alter while he was in a trauma room. Bill and Erika would leave the reunion and Bill would remember life lessons he'd forgotten over the years.

It was one of the proudest moments in my life when I typed **"The End"** to my book. When it came time to take credit for my work about a page torn from my life, I developed a strong negative reaction. I forgot I had a deep rooted fear to this story and my past. I developed the pen name "Christian Price" out of a protective instinct. The fear had been planted in my life when I was trying to recover from this near fatal shooting. My life had been delivered and transformed and I wanted to rejoice I was alive. In the same way the blind man was greeted I was greeted by an air of hostility. I survived an act society struggles to whisper let alone try and come to terms with my *"extreme method of attempting suicide."*

It started to bother me I was ashamed of my own books content. I was given a second chance at life and couldn't undo my suicide. From the moment I told the voice I wanted to be a dad I wanted to live my life. Yet, it seemed at every turn in my life someone had an opinion of suicide and me. I felt like I'd become a poster child for so many people's personal objections towards suicide; though, I hadn't been suicidal in years or decades. I'd been a recipient of a certain attitude from many people through my life. I knew the sting of this attitude I didn't know it actually had a name to it. When it comes to issues regarding mental illness and suicide there is a destructive stigma surrounding it. Anyone's life touched by suicide will come in contact with this attitude over time because suicide is nothing short of social leprosy. As I looked over the last twenty six years of my life and how I've been treated it'd made perfect sense why seeing my name on a book about me shooting myself would cause me a tremendous amount of anxiety in my life.

My first book was a week old when I sent a random email to a person whom lost a loved one to suicide. She'd started a support group for families who lost a loved one from the same battle that'd nearly taken my life. I was encouraged by the compassion she demonstrated towards people touched by suicide. In my life's travel since childhood, compassion wasn't something I'd seen a lot of as a person who survived suicide by the narrowest of margins. This was the first time I'd ever seen a support group for people traumatized and stigmatized in the aftermath of suicides storm. She responded to my email and sent me a link to her outreach and for the first time I found dozens of families familiar with the same sting I experienced through my life. Though they didn't choose to make their bed in the world of suicide they'd been thrust into it when one treasured from their life lost their battle to suicide. Suicide not only took the life of their loved one but it left a mark on their life as a consequence of their loved ones actions. They were guilty by association in the court of public ignorance. The families expressed emotional toil and exhaustion from burdens heaped upon them. Their deceased loved one was hidden by a *"curtain of suicide"*. Many of the survivor's circles of friends, coworkers, neighbors and even close family members were unable to see through the suicide to a human on the other side. It wasn't uncommon for a grieving survivor to *hear "Oh, they died by suicide."* As if a suicide related death changed something. Not that a human is suffering a profound absence from their life. Some survivors were offered "helpful" advice on how to cope with their loss perhaps a time limit on how long it was normal to grieve a loss. As if the loved one's absence were nothing more than a bad dinner buffet experience. Many of them had the same shared experience, *"Surely (dad, mom, friend, child, sibling) wouldn't want you to continue on like this? How much longer will you continue to carry this torch?"* When life is impacted from suicide it takes no prisoners and shows very little mercy.

I've been told at certain points in my life *"people are afraid of you"*. People are afraid of what they don't understand, and I'm locked in a body covered in scars from my battle with it. People's personal fear and objections of what I'd survived turned into a prison without walls. When I was in the hospital I was told *"it would've been better for you if you'd lost your legs in an accident or been burned in a fire. People can at least see those scars and be more understanding of you. They'll never understand or see your scars."* Life in prison is fierce. There's no mercy or compassion found behind its walls. There were no guide books handed out to me and very few survived what I'd done so there were no mentors to show me around to this world I'd found myself a part of. There'd be no support network when I was sent reeling from comments telling me to aim higher next time or why didn't I chose a larger caliber weapon. On occasion I was given advice on how to not "botch" the next suicide attempt. Some told me *"You must've not wanted to die."* Some of these comments I'd received before I'd graduated high school. I felt like I'd been diagnosed with a terminal illness. The healthcare community told my family chances were high I'd try again and probably succumb to it eventually because each failed attempt raises odds of future attempts. Few believed I wanted to live and if I wanted to die I wouldn't have taken that step towards life after going through the ordeal of shooting myself to begin with.

Others admitted to me they've struggled with life's depression as we sat in a safe environment where an open discussion about life is acceptable. One moment were sharing a common ground about what it is to be human when they feel they must distance themselves from me with this comment *"I've also faced the same problems as you but I **never** resorted to shooting myself."* I was judged weak because I wasn't able to handle the affairs of my life without *"actually trying to kill myself."*

I've sought career opportunities and my suicidal past was painted within the brush as possessing a criminal past. Some employers in an effort to sift through applicants post a series of questions on their applications: "Have you ever been convicted of a crime in the past?" Not far from this question and many times it was posted on the same page this question prevented me from moving forward, *"Have you ever been treated for a mental illness in the past?"* also *"Have you ever attempted suicide in the past?"* I'm unable to conveniently forget the past because the scars always call me out from behind any effort at hiding my past when my shirt comes off. My childhood dream was to be a police officer and I tried over twenty times to get my foot through the door, and because of the past, *the door remained forever closed to me.* People have laughed at me when a door wouldn't open *"You don't really expect them to give you a gun. You may shoot yourself again!"* Though the shooting happened ten years in my past when I was a teenager, it didn't matter because if you shoot yourself and survive you are forever broken in the eyes of many. My childhood dream burned away like the morning mist. Many times I was spared the effort of even knocking on the door because there was sign posted on the door, *"past history of mental illness and or hospitalizations for suicide attempts, don't bother knocking."*

When I was recovering in the hospital while hooked up to pumps and drains, I was told I needed to make up a story how I was shot in an effort to protect myself. I told people I fell on a rifle while hunting. On some occasions when I was younger some shrewd listeners would follow along and ask me to reenact the story, *"Now, how exactly did you fall on the gun?"* I felt like a total fool demonstrating this fictitious story. Based on some of my experiences with the made up story it would've made little difference if I told them the lie or truth because even this was met with jeers *"Well, remind me to stay out of the woods with you and a gun."*

Sometimes, the truth would get past me and I'd have just a brief moment to try and tell them why I intentionally shot myself one inch from my heart. This is typically the question people ask of people who end their own lives. *"Why on earth would you do something so crazy as to go and shoot yourself?"* Many times I'd spent a few moments kicking myself for not being more careful with my past and letting it get me. I was no longer a productive and trusted member of society but a dark and disturbed individual with an extreme suicidal history. It didn't matter if tried to answer why I sought to end my life when I was a teenager because the verdict was already in. Some made up their mind about my life without hearing any of the testimony and none of the facts were ever admitted in the court of public opinion. I was guilty of being untrustworthy with my own life.

I understood and can articulate why seeing my name James L. Atkisson on the cover to "When an Angel Intervenes" caused me a tremendous amount of painful anxiety. I'd have to admit that I loaded the rifle and pulled the trigger and not Christian Price. While all of my life I'd been trying to protect myself from many of the reactions I have written of and more. It wasn't until I finished "When an Angel Intervenes" did I realize I'd pried off a lid to a box I closed twenty years before. The first book was the pry bar and this book was the door to my past. Looking back twenty years wiser much of my life started to make sense, but at the time, it seemed like I was adrift at sea during a violent hurricane and my engine was dead in the water. I was at the mercy of the sea.

One of the personal benefits I received for prying the door open to my past, I started a personal healing process. As I started to look over old files in my memory box I came across an old pain that bothered me for the better part of five years after the shooting. I was told, *"Your shooting was a cry for help."* I never understood why this comment would bother me, rub me wrong or hurt and damage my self-esteem. One common held belief in our culture the best medicine for healing is we should move on almost as fast as we can and not "dwell" on the past. Based on my experience if what we are moving forward from contains misconceptions, we are sowing bad seeds with good seeds and we will get a bad harvest in our lives. What I did that day was no cry for help because I blew past that exit months before. At times it sounded like I was trying out suicide to see if I liked the fit or not. I had every intention of taking my life that night but I saw something after pulling the trigger and realized I made a dreadful and possible irreversible mistake.

When I started listening to suicide's promises my will to live started popping flares as I frantically started sending distress signals letting my society know something was terribly wrong. The thought I used a rifle to call out for help placed an enormous burden on my back as if I didn't value my life enough to fight for my own life. When people use a firearm in an effort to end their life they are committed to suicide's process.

From the first day I started to hear what suicide tried to promise me, I spoke openly of a future without me. I became obsessed with death. I gave things away and became reckless. My grades collapsed and superficial cuts started showing up on my arms. My behavior became erratic. From the first moment I started to plan suicide in June 1985 to the moment I loaded the rifle a window of seven months had passed. For years I felt poorly about myself. What kind of person wakes up one day has an impulsive thought and says *"Today I feel like shooting myself so people will notice me?"* Society wanted me to put this past me so bad seed got mixed in with good seed and an undesirable harvest occurred in my life as a result of just moving on before I was ready to move on.

There've been conversations with people who've been suicidal at different times in their life and they've understood this wasn't a cry for help. They have said to me *"you're the real deal."* I've had moments when someone is being open with me about a failed attempt and an effort to be honest I openly share my personal experience with suicide. The mood would darken and I could tell they were looking for the nearest exit. They shared with me they had only tried suicide but had never gone to the extremes I did. I remember when I only "tried" suicide in the past and when my cry went unnoticed I moved on to a very lethal attempt and only survived by a few minutes and less than an inch.

Another healing moment surfaced as a result of my writing about my past that caused me damage to my life. A person has seen me troubled and given me the courtesy of a listening ear. They were shocked I was still in pain and they'd tell me they've had similar pains in their life but they've always coped. They urge me to not play the victim and minimized the actual traumatic event as if it were an everyday occurrence. What I wanted to tell them but never had the chance was the flashbacks, nightmares, phantom smells and taste of gun powder, fear of the woods, body tremors and seeing the muzzle flash are not a typical everyday occurrences. They are scars from an encounter with a violent life or death traumatic event I narrowly lost my life to. The emotional pain post trauma stress has done to my life did more damage than the reason why I shot myself ever did. I never understood why I found this attitude troubling until I discovered what Post Traumatic Stress Disorder is and what it does to the person living with it.

Many times the question why is asked after a person has died by suicide but few to little answers are left behind. No suicide is ever the same and each person has their own reasons why. I can only share my story and why I chose suicide as the way to release myself from a decade of depression, fear and despair. No suicide is the same and personal journeys vary as there are suicides every day. I don't think it's a far leap in logic to assume I shared some similar experiences with others as we sought the same outcome.

I found the will to live is not easily dismantled and is not done on a whim. I did value my life but the white hot depression burning in the center of my mind made it impossible for me to see a few months into the future let alone years into the future. Many have strongly opposed me as though I were guilty of a crime against them personally for not thinking of my family, friends and community. When I've discussed my suicide over the last two decades this has always been one of the major flashpoints in the discussion. *"What were you thinking? Why don't people think of their family before they do something like that?"* I can't speak about other people's suicides only from my personal experience and all I can say suicide lied to me and it felt like I was under the effects of a chemical. It told me the people I knew would be better off without me and I was a burden to them. It sounds impossible to believe, but when you're under the influence of a chemical, people have a tendency to believe things they wouldn't believe if not for the chemicals influences.

I had a moment of regret. If there's anything to be taken from my story, I hope it's this thought: The moment I pulled the trigger, saw the muzzle flash, and exposed myself to a nightmare, I understood I'd been deceived.

The lie told me I could set myself free from the pain and yet when the full force of the violence enveloped my body, it broke the spell it had over my life. The lie only served to deliver me into the jaws of a beast and left me on my own from that moment. Like a powerful storm blowing away a heavy humid day and leaving behind fresh air this violence blew away the depressed spirit from my mind long enough for me to regret what I'd done. I'd take a hundred reasons why I had considered suicide if I could have another day to live. I was very fortunate and these odds should never be banked on when the stakes are so high. I'd encourage anyone that hears this seductive lie to seek out proper mental health care. Psychiatrist, licensed Psychologist, contact crisis hotlines and make it a point to interrupt the lie and fight for life.

YOU HAVE A BROTHER

I was born a month and half after the Apollo 11 crew walked on the moon during the summer of 1969. My parents were young and married at the time of my birth. My father was in the service and for the most part, I was a happy and healthy baby. My father came from a large family and I have many fond memories of spending time with my uncles, aunts and cousins. On my mother's side of the family it was small in comparison to my father's side. I had an aunt and uncle with no cousins. I had two grandparents and enjoyed spending time with them.

My grandparents lived in a small home with my aunt and uncle along with a terrier type dog. They had a very nice backyard with plenty of room for me to play. They had a very narrow driveway with just barely enough room to open a car door without hitting the house next door. When you opened the side door to the house, there was a musty odor coming from the basement.

My uncle had a large display of trophies and I used to like to sit and gaze at his accomplishments. My aunt was still in high school, and she really spoiled me with hugs and kisses. My grandfather was a heavy smoker and I can still hear the sound of his raspy cough, but I loved my grandfather and I was named after him. My grandmother managed a small convenience store. I remember their voices the smell of their home, coughing spells and the name of the small dog but I can't remember any details about my mother. One day she was gone, and with her absence she took all of her family with her. I didn't just lose my mother; I lost an entire family tree when she left. I'm not sure what day, month or year she left me or even why she left. She did come back and visit me for a week and took me to visit her family so I could see my grandparents. The house smelled the same, they had the dog and my aunt had graduated high school. I remember the visit with my mother's family and the gifts her family gave me but I can't remember one detail about my mother and her life with me.

A snapshot moment is captured to remember for decades into the future. A small boy around three years old at the time is the subject of the snapshot. The snapshot is taken to remember the moment decades into the future. The setting of the picture shows its winter because the boy is bundled up, the sun is low in the horizon and there are no leaves on any of the trees. Our hero is perched atop a slide and is peering down with a smile from ear to ear. The expression on his face shows he feels safe, secure and in love with the person taking the picture. Though many details in the picture tell a story and there are at least two people in that moment in time the snapshot reveals only one person.

I can remember that moment in the park, but my mother is not there with me. I remember the details of the park and how cold it was, but that's all I remember. If there were a second snapshot taken of this moment by a different photographer from a different location, based on my memory of the moment, the boy would be looking down into an empty space. From the memory snapshot version, it looks as if pair of scissors cut and remove the adult taking the snapshot so her memory is gone from my life forever. The child and background are there but that's all there is in the picture.

This is what my memories of my life and time with my mother consist of. Anytime I have a memory where a parent should be: a park, restaurant, swimming pool, car rides, having meals served to me, there's no one with me. I have evidence at one point in my life I had a mother but when I look for pictures of her in my mind she's gone. I'm at a swimming pool with a little girl and her mother but I'm there by myself. I have a bowl of cereal but no one there to share it with. A glass of water is handed to me by an unseen person while I ride in a car by myself. I'm at restaurants by myself and a public swimming pool unattended. Whoever I'm sharing these moments with they've been cut away to never be remembered again.

I have wonderful memories of her family and only visited them from time to time. But the person I shared a chapter of my life with and the one who gave birth to me I've no clue what she looks or sounds like. Through my life I was aware I couldn't remember her and I always assumed it was the passage of time and its effects on my memory. I never thought much of it.

One particular detail I remember she has very pretty handwriting because she sent me a letter when I was nine. From the time she left, I kept a porch light on for her in anticipation she'd eventually come back for me. When other adults spoke poorly of her I'd defend her honor. I never gave up on her and there was neither a day nor night I didn't look out the front window to see if she was pulling up in her car. When the letter came in the mail it felt like she'd been gone a lifetime because I was four when she left and the letter came when I was nine. For a nine year old boy, that was half of his life without his mother. The letter came on a hot summer day and I tore open the envelope expecting the letter to say she was making arrangements to come see me. There were two lines that changed my life, *"You have a brother... and maybe someday you can come visit us."* This was my first contact with her in years and this is what she sent me. In my logic it was easier to replace me than make a place for me and I was only worthy of a visit. Even the best case scenario was *"**maybe**"* I could come and visit with her one day. I had just finished "When an Angel Intervenes" when I was staggered by the realization I could remember her family down to small details like the name of the small dog. I don't remember if her letter hurt me but I know she is gone from my memories and, in seven years, I would hold a rifle on my body and pull the trigger.

There is one memory I have early on when my parents were separating and going through divorce proceedings. My parents were separated and lived at two separate addresses. It was a city and my mother lived in a high rise apartment complex. It was early morning hours with the sun just coming up, and my father had gone to see her. He left me alone in the car to sleep while he ran in to see her. Dressed only in pajamas and a pair of slippers for my feet I woke up to an empty car in a large urban parking lot. I recognized the apartment complex as the one my mother lived in, and I got out of the car and started towards the building. As I walked through the front door I saw her elevator and walked up and reached up as high as I could and hit a button. The elevator car came down and the door opened and I walked in as the door shut and took me to a floor. The door opened to a floor. I got out and started to wander down hallways hoping to find my parents. I'm not sure how long I wandered up and down the hallway looking but I came to a stop in front of an apartment that looked like my mother's apartment so I walked up to the door and knocked on it. Expecting to see my mother open the door I was shocked to see a man I didn't know open the door. I asked him if I could see my mother and he told me to come inside because she was inside the apartment. He held the door wide and motioned for me to come inside, but the hair on my neck stood up as a thought went through my mind. If my mother was in that apartment, then why didn't she come and greet me? I felt like the man was lying to me and he kept beckoning for me to come inside, and I had an urge to run away from this door.

Out of the corner of my eye coming down the hall I saw a uniformed police officer. My slipper had fallen off in the lobby and my father discovered it and happened to come across an off- duty police officer coming home from work. I'll never know if the man had wrong intentions or not, but I know my mother wasn't there. I remember my feet planted firmly and there was an invisible hedge between myself and this man while the hair on my neck told me something was wrong. Then a police officer was provided for me to direct me to my mother's real location.

Even though I cannot see my mother in my memories it doesn't mean she wasn't there providing for me in one way or another because the fruit of her effort bears witness she was a part of my life. Likewise, I'm unable to see the One that led me from the woods and summoned help for me. He restored my life back to my body and though I don't see Him with my eyes, I know His love for me is a testimony that His promises are true and they have the power of life within them.

A SEED IS PLANTED

Though I can't remember my mother during those days, I do remember my father. I can remember going out to dinner with him. I remember going swimming with him in the community pool as I held onto the side of the pool and watched him read a book while he rested in a lounge chair. There were pony rides, dime operated rides in front of supermarkets and days of him coaching little league baseball. He was a single dad doing the best he could with what he had.

My mother faded away while 'friends' of my father's cycled through my life. I spent days with one babysitter and nights with another. Twelve months before, life had been stable and grounded but this new life was unsteady and roaming by comparison. Some morning the bed I woke up in was not the same one I'd laid down the night before. My father was trying to balance the responsibilities of a fulltime job, time at home and pursuit of a social life.

Eventually, one 'friend' stuck around longer than others and she was not hushed out of the house like a secret and soon my dad and I relocated to a new home. This new home didn't have my mother's touch, smell or feel. The 'friend' became a permanent fixture around the home and soon her friends and family came to visit me and my father in our new home. I started to see the 'friends' family more than my father's family and this was confusing. I was no longer a part of my mother's family while my father's family was being erased from my life. The 'friend' had a large family like my father's. The adults in this family were all friendly, and the kids were polite towards me. Despite their intentions, they were not my family. I already had a mom and didn't want her replaced or anyone trying to fill her role in my life. The kids in the 'friends' family had a grandmother like I did. She was a pleasant person who tried to make me feel at home with her grandchildren. I missed my grandmother dearly and spending time with this 'grandmother' made me miss my real one that much more. Not only was she not my grandmother, she was also very different that anyone I'd ever met in my short life. She asked me routinely if I knew God His son Jesus. She asked me if my parent's had ever taken me to church. Whenever I visited her, I observed her set aside time during the day to read and study her bible. She openly asked my father the same questions she asked of me, and he waved her off and teased his 'friends' about how religious she was. Though I thought she was odd I did listen to her carefully and her words were used to plant a seed in my life. This seed one day produced a life sustaining tree I used to throw my life around in hopes it would stand up under the force I unleashed into my body.

One day my father took me to my uncle's home and left me there for a few days as he and the 'friend' left together for a few days. When they returned the friend was now my father's wife. I was six, and it was sometime during this period my mom came to visit me for a week. When she brought me back my father's wife told me, "Your mother speaks poorly about your manners and feels we aren't doing enough with you." She further told me, "Your mother is embarrassed of you." When my mother dropped me off following this visit and for several years following this visit, I was frequently reminded how embarrassed my mother was of me. As if to say to me: *"Save your breath because your mom is never coming back for you. She has washed her hands of your life."*

One day my father's wife took me to a fast food restaurant and purchased a meal for me. The meal consisted of a hamburger and a small order of French fries. The hamburger had minced onions on it. I didn't like onions. The French fries were good as always but I wasn't going to touch the hamburger while it was covered in onions. I refused to eat the hamburger as she drove and strongly urged me to eat it. I felt my life had been turned upside down in such a short manner of time. There was nothing I could do about it except just go along with the flow of the rivers current, even if this current took me to a place I didn't want to go to. I couldn't control anything. My mother was no longer in my life and with her absence her family was missing as well. It wasn't my choice to see my father's family less than what I'd been used to and certainly not my choice with regard to just being uprooted and planted in another family when I was still at a loss with what happened to my family in the first place. There was very little I had control over in my life but I could control if I ate this hamburger or not. I threw the hamburger on the floor and defiantly crushed it under my foot. I was called a brat and forced to eat the hamburger I'd crushed. Over the years my father's wife bragged how she'd won this battle of wills over a hamburger as my life started to catch on fire.

A short time after they were married, my new family moved into a neighboring town. It was at this time I noticed my father's wife's belly growing. A brother or sister would soon join me. While everyone was *"excited for me"*, I was apprehensive I was going to lose my father to another child as I'd lost my mom. Further adding to my growing emotional distress my father's wife insisted I call her *"mom."* She told me she was doing all of the work my mother should be doing for me, and if I didn't call her mom, she was going to ignore me until I stopped calling her by her first name. The term "Mom" was sacred and not a name I could just surrender to someone, who in their opinion, the time had come for me to just get over my *mom* and let go of her. The sheer weight of the grief and sadness from mother's absence told me how vital her relationship with me was supposed to be. Like crops withering in a record drought, I was starving for a nurturing relationship. In my mind I was unworthy of such a relationship. One day I'd been sick and was staying with my new grandmother for the afternoon. I was on the phone with my father's wife when the phone went silent. There was still a connection, but I knew she was dragging it out of me. If I didn't call her mom she'd continue to ignore me and since I saw her more than my dad I was going to be alone I thought. I'd been a cheerful little guy who cherished his mother and her family but one day someone took it away from me without a word. The word **"mom"** fell from my mouth and hit the floor with the weight of a collapsing brick wall.

The summer after my brother was born my father introduced a new term into my life when he started calling me *"sissy."* I wasn't sure what a sissy was, but whatever it was, my father thought it important he beat it out of me. So he signed me up for football. By this point in my life my self-perception consisted of: I was an embarrassment to my mother, a brat to my step mother and in my father's eyes a sissy that needed to have "real boys" knock it out of him.

I remember the day I learned to ride a bike. I'm not sure of the exact day on the calendar, but I can say it was during the summer months, and my new family had made plans to go camping at a popular destination. My father was impatient and started to motivate me through insults. After a period of time he gave up and tossed my bike into a dumpster. My- step mother came out and removed the bike from the dumpster and brushed it off. He came out and yelled at me, *"If you don't learn to ride the bike before we leave. I'm taking the bike with us and I'll make you ride it over the rocks."* He went back inside and left me outside alone to my thoughts.

The campsite we were using created access roads by spreading gravel throughout the campsite. From my point of view the gravel make up of these roads could have passed for implements of war during the dark ages. Individual gravels appeared to be as big as my fist and rigged with jagged edges with each having the capacity to rip skin from bone when I crashed. The crashes were a certainty because I couldn't keep my balance on a smooth and predictable black top road let alone an unforgiving shifting gravel road. The question I had to ask myself: Which one of my extremities was I prepared to sacrifice on the gravel road? At this point in my life, I'd become accustomed to many unpleasant emotions: despair, depression, anger and confusion and for the first time in my memory I was fearful of bodily harm at the hands of my father.

I did a quick calculation and figured one crash across the gravel equaled a dozen crashes over the blacktop surface. So, from where I stood there would be less wear and tear on my body if I hit the black surface a dozen times compared to one spill across the gravel. I climbed back on my bike and started to pedal. I wobbled, weaved and maneuvered the best I could and probably looked more like a new born colt trying to find his legs at birth than a boy trying to learn to ride a bike. There were spectacular crashes. I'd get back up and clean myself off and started to keep count. I figured I was still ahead of the game at this point and I had not equaled one spill over the dreaded rocks. I ran into cars, dumpsters, and smashed into curbs with narrowly missing sensitive areas. At one point there was a violent decent to the bottom of a hill followed by a fierce crash. I got out from underneath the bike with determination and pushed my bike back up the hill to try and again.

Suddenly it clicked in my head; the pedaling and balance were in harmony. I avoided cars, dumpsters and curbs. I learned how to use my foot to break and not gravity. In no time I was riding a bike and it felt like I was flying. I was so proud of my battle scars on my bike and body because they were earned in my resolve to win the battle.

During the summer a popular television show was on. It was about a man who was in a terrible accident and top rated scientist put him back together with machine parts. He was faster than what he used to be and very strong. He was put in service in fighting crime and protecting the country. It was my favorite show on television and I wanted to be like him. I reasoned if he could have those amazing parts when they put him back anyone could have those parts including me. I wanted to run and jump as he did. I wanted to fight crime and participate in top secret missions all summer. In front of our home was a bus stop and I thought all I needed was an accident then I could be like my hero because he'd been in an accident the day he got his machine parts. One afternoon, I was outside by myself and I saw a bus approaching the bus stop. I marched up to the sidewalk and watched the bus roar closer and closer approaching its usual stop. That day there was no one waiting at the stop and I thought if the bus hit me than they would put those parts in my body.

The bus approached and suddenly I heard a different voice in my head and it reasoned with me. It was a stern adult voice and it told me what I saw on TV wasn't real. There was no hero with machine parts and this bus would hurt me in a very bad way. I'd never be able to run and play and I was to **not** step out into the street. Just like in the hallway, that day, my feet were held firmly in place and I could've spit gum on the side of the bus as it drove past me. The grimy white bus roared past me without so much a hair harmed on my head. I was shaken by what my mind had been considering but very thankful for the sudden adult reasoning that interrupted my naïve childlike thinking and warned me of the danger.

I did meet a real hero one day. The one on television was imaginary but this hero was real and was in my school's auditorium. He wore a uniform, badge and carried a gun. He drove a neat car with lights, sirens and radios. People looked up to him in my community and he caught bad guys making the world a better place for us to live. We wrote letters and drew pictures to thank the police man for his time when he came out to see us. I knew when I grew up I wanted to be like him.

It was also during this time I required a surgical intervention. The surgeon was in a rural county hospital near our suburban community. He was very tall and had red hair. He made me laugh with his loud booming voice. Despite his towering frame, I felt at peace with him. What I had no way of knowing, in ten years, I would need this doctor to save my life.

YOU'RE A LITTLE LIAR

A year after my brother was born, we moved across town. It was a nice townhome community, and there were a lot of boys my age to spend time with and things for us to do. We rode bikes, played in the sandbox and tossed the football in the common area. The community had a very nice swimming pool to cool off during the summer too. With a new community always came a new school. I was in the first grade and enrolled in my third elementary school. I was having a hard time with the class work so there were "special" classes for me to attend with a few other kids. There were small behavior issues showing up in school as well. Time was spent dragging my desk out into the hallway so as to be isolated from the other kids after disrupting class. There were fights on occasions, and our teachers took us into an empty conference room to fight. I can remember fighting other kids and while we grappled on the floor the teacher sat on a desk with arms folded casually observing with as much interest as a bored emperor presiding over a gladiator contest below his balcony seat. The only thing missing was a slave offering figs and waving palm branches to cool his brow from the midday sun.

I also started to steal things from stores and other kid's homes. Nervous habits started showing up. To release stress I started to chew holes in my shirt collars and twist my finger through my hair and knot my hair up at times. I would then cut the knot out with a pair of scissors and if I couldn't find scissors I would yank the knot out from my scalp with my hand. I was told to stop doing this but it released tension from my body and I continued the nervous habit. One time a ball of hair was discovered and to avoid being in trouble I lied about the hair being mine. I was called a "little liar" and back handed with enough force to cause me to stagger back a step. My memory is not who back handed me, but more of the site of a backward facing hand followed by stars exploding into my field of vision.

Chewing on my shirt collar was the drug of choice when in class and many collars had holes in them. The teacher who permitted us to fight told the other kids he had visited my home and had dinner with us. He told the class my family served a nice steak dinner, but I was served up a plate of shirt collar. The kids laughed at me and I was angry because he lied about being at our house. I went home and told my parents about him lying to the class, and they told me he was doing me a favor. When my teacher lied about being at my house causing people to laugh at me he was doing me a favor but if I lied I was severely backhanded with enough force to make me stagger backwards.

I was jealous of my brother. My step mother told me more times than what I wanted to hear how he had developed faster than me. She would often tell me how fast he was potty training and unlike him when she met me I was still messing my pants. I was considered a brat, a liar, a sissy and not capable of using the toilet correctly while my mother complained about me behind my back. My brother was hugged, kissed and praised since he had a mother and father. He had grandparents that had terms of endearments for him meanwhile, I was nothing *"more than a lying sissy brat the messed his pants."*

The only time I felt safe and at peace was when I rode my bike or spent time with a core group of buddies. We played electric football, went to the playground and spent time in the sandbox enjoying one another's company. My 8th birthday party was a happy day. It was late August and instead of a hazy hot day the day's weather was perfect. I have a picture of that day and I treasure it because I was surrounded by friends. They came to see me and there was a group picture as they stood around me with their arms around my neck.

It seemed to me my fathers' mood started to change during this time. We had our last good memories those days. We saw movies, ate popcorn and spent time together. He took me fishing, and this was always a treat. We would start the morning with some chocolate milk and go rent a boat for the day. I enjoyed seeing the geese glide across the lake and the smell of the morning mist in the air. My father was a dad during those moments and he spoke softly so as to not scare the fish. When I was growing up, there were times I begged for him to take us to the lake so we could spend time together, but there were always more important things that needed to be done.

Just as days of fishing became less, days like one particular Saturday spent in his study became the new normal for my life. He had been yelling at me for what seemed like a long time. The room went green and when I woke up I was in my bed. I don't remember why he was yelling at me or why I passed out. I also became familiar with the belt during those days. I learned how to blunt the impact of the belt against my body. By experience, I learned how to adapt to his sessions with the belt. I knew if I wore a couple pair of pajama bottoms the blows wouldn't be as bad. Sometimes the pajama shirt would lift too high and he would get me on the back. There were times he'd inform me of his intent to whip me before I went to bed. I would have to contemplate this for a few hours, and I can remember lying in the bath and wanting to disappear into the drain.

From this point onward there are almost no happy childhood memories other than Christmas time. My family moved again midway through the fall semester of my third grade year, and I started my fourth elementary school.

ISOLATION

While I was growing up, my friends and family knew me as "Jimmy." I remember the day when I hated the name and thought by changing my name to Jim I could shed some of my history and forget my suicidal past. "When an Angel Intervenes" a few of my childhood memories are told through the character of Billy. We moved away from a suburban community into a very rural area. The nearest town with a hospital was fifteen miles away where I had my first surgical intervention a few years prior.

Gone was the town home complex with a group of friends to toss the football with. No more swimming pool or play-ground with its large sandbox. Instead of electric football contest with other boys, I was given the woods to play in by myself. I was used to people and activity, but I stood on the porch to my new home and was shocked how quiet and lifeless this rural area was compare to where we moved from. My father and stepmother appreciated the quiet but I was in shock and hated it. While I was changing elementary schools frequently my brother and I also changed day care providers with as much frequency. My step mother's mother had been a steady and safe place for my brother and me to go for daycare. For reasons I don't know she was unable to continue to watch us so we bounced around from home to home. When we moved to the rural area, I was in the third grade and a latch key child for a while. I would only need the services of a day care provider over the summer breaks or on holidays. This provider had two teenage sons and from my point of view, they were as large as grown men.

One day at the day care provider's home for reasons I'll never know, the baby sitter grabbed me and threw me on the floor and sat on my back. While she sat on my back she passed gas on me in front of her two sons who thought the spectacle was the funniest thing they'd ever witnessed. In an effort to defend myself from being violated, I fought back by hitting her. This made her jump up to her feet. Her sons yanked me to my feet and man handled me around the room briefly for striking their mom. When my stepmother came to pick me up that afternoon, the sitter complained to her that I'd punched her. She never bothered to fess up to what she did to me. I had felt confident when I defended myself my family would agree with me that I had acted properly. The baby sitter denied everything, and my stepmother believed the baby sitter over me. It was a long drive back home as I knew I'd be punished for supposedly lying once more and hitting the baby sitter. As I looked out the back window of the car I dreamed of flying away and escaping this home.

I also suffered terrible asthma attacks as a child. One summer morning, I was having a terrible attack when I was dropped off at this provider's home. The day was hazy, hot and very humid. I was told I had to spend the day outside and not indoors in the air-conditioning. The baby sitter told me my parents didn't want me in the house even if the air-conditioner did help my breathing.

The only time I was permitted in the house was to use the bathroom and lunch. I spent the day in the back yard laying in a folded out lounge chair trying to breathe. All day it felt like a hundred pound sack was in the center of my chest and I was trying to breathe through a drinking straw. I remember watching my belly rise and collapse trying to push the trapped air in my lungs out of me. It felt like an invisible hand was over my nose and mouth trying to suffocate me. I knew the cool and comfortable air conditioner would help me relax and I'd be able to breathe easier. She wouldn't let me in the house and she'd come to the sliding door and watch for a few minutes and leave. Through the day my breathing grew worse, and I knew if I panicked it would make it worse. I focused on exhaling long and slow trying to force the air back out of me. There would be times I'd drift off to sleep from exhaustion. The ordeal went on throughout the day, and I can remember talking to God that day. When my step mother came to pick me up I'm not sure if she said anything to this day care provider, but I knew by the time we rode the thirty miles back home, I was bad off. I lay in my bed while my step mother sat next to me with a cool washcloth over my forehead. The next day when I woke up I could breathe, and my room was full of a golden glow from the morning sun. The only reason why I knew I was still alive was I noticed the washcloth next to my body from the night before.

It was at this point in my life I received the letter from my mother when she wrote me *"...maybe I could come for a visit."* I knew she was never going to come back for me. I believed in her and argued she'd never quit on my life but she did. She had a new son and perhaps I could visit her while he lived with her. In my mind at the time, I wasn't her son anymore. I was a potential guest and the fool for believing in her. I was starting to get angry at the way life was treating me. While her son was with my mom I'd laid in a back yard and nearly suffocated to death while the adult who violated me watched with no concern. I told the truth but I was the liar. All of my families were for the most part gone. I was afraid of my father, and I was not as fast at picking things up compared to my brother. I wasn't ten years old and thought my life had as much value as the roadside garbage set out once a week.

My father spent some nights yelling at my stepmother and my stomach would hurt as I heard her crying. The arguments were usually centered on money and his relationships with other women. My father had turned into a person that if he wanted something he would take it. If he wanted to buy something he didn't care if it came from bill or grocery money, he would buy it anyway. The walls were thin in the house so I could hear the arguments and I would hear him brag to his wife about how different women wanted to spend time with him. The tension was always very high as result of these destructive arguments. As the years went on, my stepmother drew a circle around her son but left me to fend for myself. I know this to be true because she told me: I was on my own.

The older I got, the longer his list of chores were for me. I went to school and I worked. For the first year or two in the new home my father was obsessed with his driveway. He purchased tons of gravel and brought some shovels and a wheel barrow. He told me we were spending time together by hauling tons of gravel around the driveway just the two of us. If my father ever wanted a break he would take a break and leave for an afternoon. While he was gone, he piled chores on me to keep me busy in his absence. My father liked to communicate through list and treated them as intercompany memos. I can count the number of fun filled family event on my two hands. We went to the beach for a day, went to a few movies and a regional amusement park a couple of times. I went to a summer camp for a week and swimming once or twice. From the time we moved away from the town home community to the day I shot myself in the chest, my life was nothing but work and discipline. When I finished with one task, he looked for more things for me to do. There was always a mountain of firewood and an expanding garden that needed to be weeded by hand. If I wasn't working I was spending time just wasting in a chair or laying in my room wandering what I ever did to anyone to be treated like this. The depression was starting to grow and there was no time to be a kid. There was a nice boy who lived across the street, and it was such a treat to visit him and his nice family. They were always kind and spoke nicely to him. He shared in family chores but he also had time to be a boy.

On a rare occasion I remember my stepmother being upset at the way my father looked at the neighbor across the street, and I knew it hurt her feelings. It made me angry he hurt her feelings and though she wasn't my mother she worked hard to take care of my brother and me, and it didn't seem right. Sometimes he didn't care if I was with him or not. He seemed to thrive on charming other women.

My father started to drink openly. It started out once or twice a year and over the years it got worse. It never affected his job and never caused any trouble for him outside of our home. This was not the same father I knew who used to sit and read a paperback while I hung on the side of pool and waved at him. There were nights he'd sit and brood over his drinks while we tried to eat dinner afraid to breathe. It was torture around the home because I didn't know if he would explode in a rage- filled, ill- temper tantrum one moment or the moment would pass without a word.

When I started junior high school a sizeable property next to my parent's home went up on the market, and my father thought it was a good investment. The property was packed with honeysuckle, saplings, poison ivy, briars and woods. From the road you could only see a stone's throw through the thick canopy of underbrush. Once my father purchased the land, he decided to cut a path through the woods all the way to a small creek sitting at the end of his new property line.

We started at the road marking the beginning of the property line and started a campaign to reach the creek. At first, the progress was measured in feet. It wasn't uncommon for me to get home from school and have to clean up from the previous night's work. When he got home from work he'd take the tools and rip things down and I would follow after him picking up the mess. Through briars, saplings, trees, and poison ivy we pushed as if we were Marines moving through the jungles of Guadalcanal during World War 2 to make paths rarely used. Once we finished cutting a path to the peaceful meandering creek, he shut the power tools down for a moment. We picked up all of the tools and marched back to the road to contemplate the thick brush covered field for a few minutes. From where we stood on the road, the start of the property marker through the densely covered field to the small creek on the other side of the property was about a quarter of a mile. The same creek, I would sit next to in the coming years and pull a trigger.

He fired up the power tools and a process was started that went on for a couple of years. When we started, the land was so thick with vegetation some days I lost my shadow. Yet, when we finished the land could've passed for the rough on a golf course. The only thing missing was the pin marking the 18th hole. When he hit large stumps or rocks, we dug them out or pulled them up with a truck. When he shut the tools off for the night many nights it looked like a tornado had touched down and moved across the land waiting for me to clean up the next day. When I got home from school it was cleaning up the mess the night before and during the weekend, it was from sunrise to sunset.

If it wasn't time out in the field, it was time on my hands and knees in the garden or hauling tons of gravel or cleaning up from many never-ending home renovations. If he wasn't yelling at me, he was shoving me or jamming an index finger into my chest. He enjoyed bragging to me how much stronger and tougher he was compared to me. Personally, I thought it was easier to make a mess of things than make things right.

One of my fathers' preferred corrective measures was "Chair Time." Time spent in the chair was time no different than solitary confinement in a corrective institution. When I was sentenced to time in the chair, my body was to sit from the time I got home from school until bed time. On weekends or holidays, it was from sun up until bed time. I could only get out of the chair when I wanted to go to the bathroom. This would often feel like I was on vacation because it would provide relief from the steel cutting into the back of my legs or the pressure on my backside. Most of my peers looked forward to spring break, Memorial Day and Labor Day, but I did not. I dreaded summer vacations and counted the days when school would begin the next fall, I was not allowed to read, play or take a nap. On occasion I did have a clock radio to keep me company. My father would tell me if I did not like my punishment I should avoid the crimes. The worst place to spend this time I found was in the kitchen because I had to sit upright for the better part of the day. There was no slouching, napping or reading when I was locked down in the kitchen. It was a treat to be shut down in my room because I learned to hide things under a desk blotter. I would often write short stories while I spent time in the chair or sneak a nap in. One day I noticed a box of map pins in the back of a drawer and couldn't believe I'd over looked them for so long. Many times, God puts treasures before our eyes we simply miss them. This box of map pins had been in there as long as the desk had been in my room; I just never saw it for what it was. The pins came in six different colors. I organized each colored pin into its color and that represented a standing army. There were gold thumb tacks who were the kings of the armies. I spent many hours engaging in epic struggles and found an escape from time in the chair through my imagination and the map pins. After spending all day in the chair, my legs had no strength in them and it felt like my rear was developing raw areas from the constant pressure of skin on metal. The worst part was the mental anguish as I watched the minutes grind down the day like a mill stone grinding grain into flour. From my bedroom window, I saw my brother play or go errands with his mother while my life wasted away.

We had a family dog and I could see her from my bedroom window. She lived outside and was tied to her dog house. She almost never came off her tie out and her life consisted of ten feet of chain. In the same way the dog was tied to the chain; I was tied to the chair or the fifty feet of brush my father had me cleaning up. On occasion the dog was released from her chain and on occasion I was released and could ride my bike or go for a ride into town.

I was caught in a whirlpool of depression and it was starting to take me under. I was being punished for issues at school or if my father just got mad. These cycles at home made it difficult to concentrate at school. Many times the pattern would consist of: I didn't do a homework assignment because though my body was counted for attendance, my mind had checked out. I would go home and tell my father I had no homework because I honestly don't remember homework being assigned. My grades would indicate the homework assignments and then I had to face harsh consequences at home.

It was not out of the ordinary to be dragged out of the bed in the middle of the night and be forced to "stand at attention" as if I were a recruit in basic training for the crime of struggling in school. Some nights he would silently chew his dinner and glare at me while I had to stand at attention within arm's reach of him. I never knew if he would explode out of his chair and shove, smack me or throw his plate of food at me. He would blame me for losing his temper. There were times I'd ask he not call me names but he would tell me, "I'm your father, I will call you whatever I want to call you."

My father drove a truck with all-weather tires, and I could hear the tires from over a mile away. I learned to hate the sound of the tires over the road because it sounded like they were coming for me. I would get a pit in my stomach because I never knew how the night was going to work out for me it was always up in the air. One Friday night, I heard the tires with their distinctive roaring sound as they drew near the house. When he came in, he eventually made his way to the front porch and called for me. He was in a bad mood and he asked to see my "idiot list". *The* "idiot list" was a special list he had created for me to take to school to show the teachers. It was a daily report card and I hated it. I hid this list from the other kids, but sometimes they would ask me about it or yank it out from my notebook. Many times there was no way to be discreet about it because I had to go to the front of the class to have it checked off.

This particular Friday I'd left the "idiot list" at school. There was an icy cold silence in the night air as he glared at me. He told me to start walking towards the school and not come back home until I had my "idiot list" with me. At first I thought he was joking, but he was deadly serious and I'd better get walking. I reminded him the school was twelve miles away, the school was closed, and it was well after dark. None of it mattered because he wanted the list home that night. My sneaker echoed through the night air as I headed out for the locked school twelve miles away. The only sound heard was the footfall and the crying coming from a broken heart. After a couple of hundred yards, he yelled down the road, "Hey, stupid come back." I was invisible to the world. My mother left without a look back. I was just sent down a dark road to get an idiot list. I'd been violated by an adult and called a liar and punished for trying to defend myself. The family dog and I shared common ground, we were both chained animals.

MARK

It was early spring and the air was rich with the smell of honeysuckle and seasoned with a hint of fresh cut grass. It was Friday afternoon and I'd been looking forward to the weekend all week. It was the first real nice spring week after the winter thaw. The television guide had advertised a good movie and I looked forward all week to the weekend and movie. My plan for the weekend was just to ride my bike. One relaxing pastime I enjoyed was just meandering around on my bike and pretend I was a World War I pilot on patrol. I liked to pretend I was in the open air cockpit flying high above the chaos of No Man's Land. It was going to be a great weekend with the movie, weather and my bike but there was a problem.

In the pocket to my pants was a report card and it was a train wreck. It screamed at me I was headed for an ugly night at home. The report card was covered with insightful remarks from my teachers and many times the remarks sent my father into orbit. There were remarks about me rarely turning in my homework and since the "idiot list" hadn't been used this marking period, I was on my own.

My mind was never in class. I'd spent more hours daydreaming in class than paying attention to the teacher. I'd spent many hours listening to the other kids and found myself very curious. What did it feel like to go out for dinner, visit family, or go to the mall for a pair of shoes? Instead of math class when the teacher was handing out assignments for the following day, my thoughts were on how wonderful it would be to live in a home where I wasn't called names. When it came time for English, I dreamt of a mom who loved me and wanted me in her life. In Biology class, thoughts were devoted on trying to imagine what it was like to live in a peaceful home.

This report card in my pocket made reference to me having done very little homework over the semester. When I got home that day my body buzzed with anxiety, and I wished for once I could skip the drama. I wanted this torment to end. When my father got home that night we ate dinner in silence. After dinner he looked over the grades and comments. The comments called me a "low achiever" and in the teacher's opinion, I was capable of much more if only I applied myself. He assumed I'd been lying to him about the grades and decided that night I'd be responsible for choosing my own punishment. My options were spend the weekend in the steel chair from Friday night until Sunday night. This meant I was going to miss the movie and not enjoy the rich weather for the upcoming weekend. The other option was he would take me out into the garage and whip me with his belt. The moment would be over in a few moments and then I could enjoy the movie and weekend. However that meant bearing up under the crack of the heavy belt. Sometimes he thought it important before he hit me with the belt to fold the belt in a loop. Then flex the belt so there was slack and then yank it so it went taught and made a very distinctive **CRACK.**

He got up and went outside and left me to my thoughts. I dreaded the belt and for a brief moment decided it would be better for me to sacrifice the movie and weekend. The minutes ticked past, and the clock told me my movie was going to be on soon. The windows were open and the fresh air found its way into my nose further reminding me I didn't want to sit in the chair for two solid days. My heroes had always been brave people from pilots to superheroes to policemen. It was my opinion if I wanted to enjoy the movie and weekend, then I needed to be brave and overcome my fear of him and his belt. So I pushed the chair back and headed outside. When I touched the back door I paused for a brief moment and did a final gut-check before I went outside to face him. With my lungs full of fresh air I was very aware of the impending moment. I opened the door, and stepped outside, and walked up to my father. I had more courage and heart that moment than the man who was about to beat me. I told him "I'll take the beating."

He told me he was proud of me and led me to the garage and shut the door. He told me to turn around and bare my back to him. I closed my eyes and dreamed of my weekend as he laid into me. I stood my ground as the grown man put everything he had into this beating for the crime of struggling in school. The garage was dark, and I could hear cars drive past on the road outside. No one was going to rescue me from my life because I was invisible to the world. The belt cut into my skin, and when he finished, he told me to get cleaned up. In the bathroom mirror I could see why he told me to clean up. The skin had been torn open. He opened the door to the bathroom and told me to tell no one.

I finished cleaning up and was very proud of myself for earning my freedom. I only missed a few minutes of the movie but that was ok because it was better than sitting in the chair and missing the entire movie. Saturday morning came and I went outside to ride my bike. He'd been busy expanding his garden and there were always rocks to clean out of the garden. As I got ready to ride my bike, he asked me what I was doing so I told him. He decided he needed my help carrying rocks out of the garden and I was to help him. There wasn't time to play because he frequently found "useful work" for me to do and wanted to "keep me out of trouble." I'd been beaten for no reason. I could've stayed in the chair on Friday and been spared the belt.

When I was writing When an Angel Intervenes this moment from my childhood was so traumatic, my writer voice wanted it in the book. I hadn't thought about this moment in over twenty years. When I wrote this scene out, it was remembered by Bill as he visits a childhood friend named "Mark". Mark is a successful free spirited businessman and Bill is a struggling contractor trying to keep the basics provided for his family. As the two men visit and catch up on old times, Bill remembers a day when he and Mark were to spend one day on their bikes. They'd made plans to meet at a certain time but Mark had to move their play date to a different time during the day. Mark explains to Billy he and his mother are supposed to spend the morning together. However it made little difference because Billy was unable to meet his friend the next day because he had to carry rocks after he was beaten the night before.

I had readers ask me about the character Mark and if he were a fictional character or a true friend from my past. When I wrote this scene out, I hadn't given Mark much thought and it wasn't until I considered a few readers' questions and started on this book that I was struck with a revelation, I never had the chance to grow out of childhood. What little of my childhood I had left died the moment I pulled, the trigger and memories of my childhood were speaking to me through the character Mark. I'd not visited my childhood in over twenty years and prior to the shooting, I used to day dream my mother would spend a Saturday with me. After the shooting, I never again day dreamed about her spending time with me because the shooting changed me.

During their conversation Mark wants to know how his friend's life turned out and Bill says, "Ok". This isn't entirely true because Bill is feeling deep emotional scars from childhood and a vague burden he's not measured up. Bill was given a second chance at life and the only thing he has to show for this gift is the pictures he carries in his wallet. While the world around Bill has pursued **more** of everything; Bill has limped along and fallen short. In Bill's opinion, he should've contributed more to this legacy so entrusted with.

I know what it is to be given the gift of a second at life. With a gift like this comes a tremendous responsibility to not squander it. As I started to move through life from one failure to another failure, I started to feel I was going to squander this precious gift. In some ways, I started to feel I wasn't worthy of this gift God had given me until I wrote <u>When an Angel Intervenes</u>. It was a key to unlocking this books content. This book started me on a journey towards an overdue healing. It made me scoot back from my life like the day when I found map pins in my desk drawer, map pins that became a treasure of imaginative adventures. I had overlooked them for so long, but they were in front of me all along.

Mark is a success in his own right as well as Bill. Billy's heart's desire was to survive that moment and grow up one day and be a dad. Bill pulls out a wallet and shows Mark a wallet full of children's pictures. His treasures were in front of him all along, but it got lost when he tried to keep up with the world. At one point, Bill is able to reassure Billy his life is more than ok just as I was able to reassure Jimmy, my life is blessed and I'm a truly rich man.

My stepmother was hurting and angry over the way her life was turning out with my father. One evening she was bathing my little brother and I thought it would be funny if I shut the master circuit breaker off to the house for a brief moment. Being young, I never stopped to consider the consequences that perhaps I may harm someone. I flipped the switch and the lights went out briefly and then I flipped the switch back on. My stepmother came into the room where the circuit break was located and found me. I was smiling because I thought it was funny. The rage in her eyes told me I was nothing more than vermin caught in a storage pantry when the lights were suddenly clicked on exposing the trapped animal. She lunged across the room and hit me hard enough to stagger me into the wall. I was sent reeling into the wall by the same person who violated and threatened to ignore me if I didn't call her mom before I'd come to terms of my biological mother was gone. However, when her son picked up a metal skillet and snuck up behind me paused to take aim then cracked me across the back of the head, this was considered funny.

She was also under a tremendous amount of stress trying to keep food in the house. My father would freely drain the bank accounts if he wanted to and spend money without regard to the household budget. She rationed me food and would close the kitchen down and forbid me from going into the kitchen to try and get something to eat. I was working outside all of the time and growing but limited how much I was permitted to eat. She would yell at me for trying to get a snack and insist she had to "make it stretch." I felt embarrassed and shameful for having to feel like I was looting or stealing from the kitchen, but I was hungry all of the time. People teased me growing up for being rail thin. She assured me I wasn't going to starve to death and I was getting enough calories. I also felt sleepy all of the time at school and many days only focused on how many hours I had to wait before the lunch bell. Some days during summer vacation the only thing my brother and I had for lunch were two slices of bread with mayonnaise and no lunch meat. When she went to the store and the groceries were gone that was all there was until the following pay day unless she had to "float" a check for a couple of days to get some groceries for her home.

By the time I started high school my mind and heart were on fire with depression. I believed my life had no more value than the dog tied up outside. Most days I went to bed hungry, tired, and fearful of my life. My only escape in life was school. When I went to school I was safe from bodily harm and not constantly doing mindless tasks one right after the other. I wasn't walled off in my room to stare at a blank wall and there was always a good lunch. I looked forward to high school because that meant the end of another summer vacation, and I could start my real vacation, life away from the house.

HIGHSCHOOL

High School started for me in the fall of 1984. There were plenty of extracurricular activities to occupy my time. I played freshmen football, marched in the band and spent time in the weight room. There was a local bible study sponsored by a Christian athletic organization and our local police department had a police cadet program for teenagers interested in a career in law enforcement to keep my interest that first year. From the first time in elementary school to the day I signed up as a police cadet I still held fast to the dream of pursuing a career as a police officer.

In my homeroom class there was a very polite and likeable girl. In no time we became friends and she reminded me of my grandmother. She openly shared with me about Jesus and how much God loved my life. She told me He wanted to be my Father and it sounded appealing, but I wasn't interested in making a commitment to Jesus at this point in my life. I was very moved at this thought God loved me because it was something I was starved for. I was impressed she was sharing with me this message because it was the same message my grandmother had shared with me almost ten years before. It seemed like God was trying to get my attention, but the last thing I wanted was to be associated with awkward Christians at school when I was already buried beneath a life of difficulty at home.

I was proud of my affiliation with the football team. I really enjoyed being part of the team and wearing my jersey to school. For the most part, I was invisible to the other kids. I rarely spoke to them in the hallways and I was never invited to any of the social gatherings. They were rarely unkind towards me because they didn't see me; I was very withdrawn and quiet. Like most teens one of my sensitive areas was my wardrobe. I had two pair of pants in my freshmen year of High School and both of them were blue corduroys. One was only darker than the other.

The financial strain was always a pressure point in the home. Much of the stress had to do with my father's constant spending splurges. He bought everything from a car, truck, tractors, tools and guns while at one point my bed consisted of a sheet of plywood for a few months and I was rationed calories many times. His temper was worse than ever going into my freshmen year of High School. One Sunday afternoon, we were cleaning out the property from the never ending underbrush. He was in a foul mood for reason's I didn't understand. When he was in these kinds of moods it never ended well for me. He climbed into his truck, and without looking, he backed up over one of his new chainsaws and bent the tool. He parked the truck, jumped out of the truck, and saw the tool. His face flashed over with rage at me. He jumped back into the truck, and it happened so fast I didn't have time to warn him. He drove other the other saw that sat not too far away. He parked the truck and got out and walked over to one of the ruined saws and picked it up. He turned and started to walk towards me with it in his arm. My stepmother was just out of arms reach. What I saw next shocked me. *He actually raised the saw up over his shoulder and started to swing it at me like a club.* As the saw came forward, my step- mother yelled at him to stop as I jumped back and out of the way. At the last minute he pulled back and the saw missed my head. It slammed into the side of his truck putting a gouge into the side of the bed. When I was six years old, I believed him to be a threat to my physical body, and when I saw the chainsaw coming towards my head, it confirmed to me he was. I wasn't the only person aware of this threat as my step-mother screamed at him to not hit me with the saw. In year and half from this point, she'd warn me of his potential danger to my life, and it would have near fatal consequences for my life.

That fall I'd been on a band trip and he picked me up from school well after sunset. It was late, and as we drove home, he started yelling at me. He wanted to know where my "idiot list" was, and I realized in haste of trying to get myself to the band room to prepare for the trip, left the list and homework in the locker at school. The road we were traveling on was a major connection from our sleepy end of the county to the more suburban area twenty miles east.   The speed limit was fifty-five and at the time of the night the road was lightly traveled. With no warning, he stopped his truck in the middle of the road just around a bend. He shut the motor off and turned the lights out. We were in the middle of the road around a blind spot with not as much as a hazard lamp blinking, and, at the time, the road was empty of traffic, but it wouldn't be for long. I was beside myself as he started to yell at me, but I never heard a word of it because I was too busy looking over my shoulder wondering how long it was going to take before an innocent driver on their way home appeared around the bend traveling at the posted speed limit and plowed into us. After a few minute he turned his truck back on and drove us home.

He'd gotten a new push mower and it would take me the better part of eight hours to push mow the acre he considered our yard. It drove him nuts it took me that long because there were more things he wanted me to get done, and he accused me of being lazy and sloppy. He said I should happily "serve" him and there was no time for recreational family time. I wasn't a son but livestock on a ranch. When I started his new mower I didn't realize he had never added oil to the engine. Engines blow without oil and this engine was no different so he grabbed me and dragged me to his garage. I assumed I was going to get another beating but instead he picked up hand shears and threw them at me and told me to clip the lawn by hand until he got a new mower. On my hands and knees, I clipped the lawn by hand until my hands could no longer squeeze the blade together.

One Saturday afternoon, he had to leave for his part- time-job and he left me with a list. His list looked like memos more than a list of things to do. He liked to initial of the bottom of the list or write on top *"from the desk of"*. It was important for him to know where I was in relation to him and this was something that never changed even into my adulthood. It was important to me to keep the peace in the house, follow the directions of his list to the letter and not deviate from it.

On that day, I was to move smaller piles of brush and put them into what constituted a master brush pile. This master brush pile sat in the center of the field I'd been toiling in for years just left of center not far from a country lane running parallel to my family's property. The master brush pile was the size of a tractor trailer, and from where my family's home was situated, it blocked the field of vision at the point of entry I routinely used to walk into the woods whenever I wanted to visit the small creek at the rear of their property. The list told me to use his truck to drive around the field and pick up the smaller piles then drive them to the master pile. I was to be done before the sun went down. It started to rain as I set out for the day in the field with the truck. The ground was soft but I got the work done like he wanted before it got dark. When I went to bed I was tired and sore but the rain beating against my window made it easy to fall asleep.

At some point during the night, he got home from work and burst into my room flipping on the light yelling for me to get up. He screamed at me to get dressed and meet him in the field. It was still raining and the cold spring air chilled my bones as I walked up to where he was standing in the field. He flipped the lights on to his truck and illuminated the two of us. He let loose a stream of vulgarities into my core. While moving the piles of brush, I'd left tire ruts through the field, but I was afraid of not getting the list done. History had taught me what happened if I didn't get the list done. Consequences may range from chair time to getting shoved. Other times, he would bury me under more work. Fear of his list would also have consequences in my life in nine months.

I had a very deep-rooted fear in not getting his list done. In the cold April rain, I listened to him rail against my life for trying to get his list done as he instructed me to do. Nine months from that night his never-ending list and verbal abuse would push me to shoot myself about a quarter of a mile away from where he was yelling at me. Just like that cold April night on Thursday, January 23rd, he gave me a very long list of things to do before he got home from work for Friday, January 24th. Instead of carrying out my assigned list, I was seated by the small creek with a rifle across my lap. At that moment in time, I was a peace of garbage whose only purpose in this life was to suffer at the hands of adults. I sat for an hour trying to work up the nerve to load that rifle and pull the trigger, but I wasn't able to bring myself to actually do it. While I squandered the hour trying to shoot myself, I wasn't completing the assigned task of the list. When I gave up and started to walk home to return the rifle, I remembered the list sitting uncompleted in my bed room, and there wasn't any point in going back to live another day. I turned and walked

back towards the small creek with the rifle in hand intent
on dying that night.

My father told me I was stupid for not having enough sense to haul the brush by hand to the master brush pile. When he finished yelling at me he told me to start marching through the field and anywhere I saw a tire rut I was to mash the rut back into the ground by foot while the ground was still soft from the rain. He shut the lights out to his truck and went back inside leaving me in the dark, rainy night to mush tire ruts back into the earth. This wouldn't be the last time tire ruts were cut into this ground. Police cars, paramedic chase cars and an ambulance would leave many tire ruts in this ground.

THE LIE BEGINS

The summer of 1985 started out badly for me. I'd received a notice the last day of school my grades were going to be held up and I couldn't advance to the tenth grade if I didn't pay for my overdue library books and damaged text books. I'd barely passed the ninth grade and barely passing was as bad as not passing at all. I panicked over this notice and decided to not mention anything to my parents about the held up grades. I figured I could enjoy a week of summer vacation before the storm hit. I even checked the mail box daily, found the notice and tossed it into the garbage before anyone had a chance to see it. I was deeply distressed what this summer would mean for my life. School had always been a safe place for me to hide from him, but here I was facing three month of intensive one on one father son time. This kind of time wasn't the going- fishing- kind of time but the kind of time that was killing me.

I'd been out of school for over a week when I felt a snap inside of my head. I felt a bout of fear and anxiety I had never felt before. My heart was racing when an animal reached into my chest with an icy claw and started to yank on my heart. As I struggled with the anxiety I paced back and forth through our home. In my travels, I walked past the room containing a gun cabinet. For a moment I thought: *"I could escape all of this if I stuck one of those guns against me and pulled the trigger."* It was an impulsive thought and it was my first step on a journey that would end in seven months. My thought process started to cast it aside as quickly as the thought injected itself into my thinking. But, I took another step down the road when I walked into the room and opened the gun cabinet to remove a firearm. It was heavy and sturdy in my hand. Adrenalin coursed its way through my body and acted as an antidote counteracting depression and despair's deadly venom. There at the bottom of the cabinet, I found the shells to the gun and pulled one out. I put the shell in the gun and closed the action. I no longer felt depressed but hope filled. I had an answer to my despaired life and it was here in my hands. Just like the hamburger I tossed on the ground, this I could control. My sense of personal welfare sounded an alarm in my head and demanded I return the gun at once. I replaced the firearm and gently closed the gun cabinet.

My father received a courtesy call at work telling him of my impounded grades so my deception was up it was time to face him. The consequences were severe as suspected and after being shoved around the house, I was confined to the chair for a couple of days. My summer vacation was over before it started and the more I considered suicide as the way to manage my pain the faster my pace went towards the goal: to be released from pain.

After setting me free from the chair, he turned my home into a work camp. My life centered on working in the field. Work started after breakfast and didn't stop until dinner. When he got home from work, I had to follow him back into the field until he thought it was too dark to keep working. There was no break unless it rained.

My grandfather was staying with us at the time, and he was under orders to keep the house door locked. I wasn't allowed inside of the house unless it started to rain. If I wanted a drink, I had to get it from the garden hose. One benefit from the constant labor was I got very fit and I could keep pace with my father unlike years in the past. I'd also been given some free weights and many days when I was finished my list for the day I'd spend the evenings using the free weights. The harder I worked the stronger and more energetic I became. By the end of the summer, I could almost outwork my father. I would need these physical reserves in five months.

One rainy day a few weeks before my sophomore year in high school, I had the day off from my list and was visiting the farm across the road from our home. There was a man who lived a few miles away from us looking to hire someone to paint his farm buildings. He was offering three hundred dollars and this seemed like a king's ransom so I agreed to the task only if my father would allow it. My father agreed and I was very excited with what I could do with three hundred dollars. There were two large barns and several smaller storage buildings needing a fresh coat of yellow paint. My family would drop me off in the mornings and pick me up on their way home from work. I would take a break to eat lunch or take a drink from the water hose. I never quit and worked like a seasoned professional painter. Within a few days the job was finished much to the man's satisfaction. I was rich man when I held my three hundred dollars cash. The first thing I did was add to my wardrobe. Still stinging from the previous year's fashion failure and only owning two pair of blue corduroy pants I went out and invested in a proper wardrobe for the upcoming year.

From the time I celebrated my 8th birthday to the time I celebrated my 16th birthday there were less than twelve family excursions away from the home. There was no life outside of school or my father's constant list. One of the ten fond memories occurred two weeks before I turned 16. I was invited to attend a church summer camp. My father was proud of the way I painted the farm so he agreed to let me go for the week. Compared to the way summer began, the end of the summer was working out very well. My suicidal thoughts had submerged from my daily thoughts at the end of the summer.

The bus was full of kids I'd never met before but they were friendly and accepting. It felt good to be away from the world I'd come to know, and at time I felt dizzy from the release of stress. There was no list taped to my door and there was plenty to eat. I wasn't called names, and when I went to the dinner hall the other kids saved a place for me. If I wanted to rest, the door to the dorm wasn't locked prohibiting me from lying down in my bunk. I felt like I was visiting another world or country foreign compared to the world I lived in. I wasn't afraid every day and worried about the atmosphere around me. I didn't always have to live in a heightened state of awareness.

I also met my first girlfriend at this camp. She had a lot of questions about my life and I was ashamed that I had nothing to brag about. I used to play football and as a consequence to the final grade point average the year before my father assumed I didn't meet the minimum standards to play. He wouldn't even consider allowing me the chance to try out so I couldn't brag to her I was a football player. The truth: I was a boy who spent the better part of his life sitting in a steel chair pushing map pins around a desk blotter pretending they were toy soldiers or hauling piles of vegetation around a vacant field. With no end in sight to her interrogating me about my mysterious life, I did what any self-respecting teenage boy would do in the face of losing the first girl to ever show any interest: *I lied.* I was ashamed of how uninspiring I was in the light of her gaze and there was nothing about my life consistent with her perceptions about me. The girlfriend moment was bitter sweet. She demonstrated what *should have* been right about my life unlike the *reality* of my life. She saw so much value in me and for the first time in memory, someone wanted me in their life. Like a swollen river spilling out of its banks, despair swept into my heart and mind on the bus trip home. The charade was over and with each mile the bus took me closer to the reality of my life and further from the respite I'd gotten from life.

The lists were ready for me when I got home and, in short order, I picked up where I left off when I went to paint the farm. One evening a few days before school started my father and I were cutting firewood when he sent me to *"fetch"* him a drink. When I was in the house the phone rang and I answered it. On the other end of the line was the athletic director from the school and he wanted to know why I hadn't been at summer conditioning and would I be ready for practice next week when school started? I wanted to drop the phone when he asked me that question. I explained to him my father's concern and his assumption I didn't qualify for football in the upcoming year. He assured me I did qualify, and he looked forward to seeing me on the team next week. I was ecstatic that I did qualify and I could play football that year. I knew the junior varsity team was thin because the varsity coach cherry- picked much of the talent, but I didn't care. It would give me plenty of playing time, and I could brush up on some fundamentals and be ready when it came time to move up to the varsity football the following year.

I hung up the phone and sprinted to where my father was busy cutting firewood, yelling and waving for him as I ran. He shut off the power tool and set it down on the ground. He was angry I didn't bring a drink back with me. I told him about the phone call, but he didn't believe me the director had called. After some convincing, he finally believed me and looked at me with disgust. He picked up his power tool and told me my grades "sucked", and the athletic director should be ashamed for allowing me on their team. He questioned their standards and in his opinion, the team was of poor quality and surely they were scraping the bottom of the barrel to fill holes in their roster. I told him under state law I qualified and it would be a great opportunity to get playing time in. He held two of his fingers just a hair with a part and demonstrated to me how close I was to being a loser. Demeaning me was his parenting philosophy. It started when I first learned to ride a bike and it went on until I was old enough to drive a car. I felt less like a son and more like an animal in the clutches of a person who derived pleasure in extracting pain from a small animal. He told me many times growing up: "I'll either make you or break you boy."

The week before I'd been a winner and had been accepted by a company of my peers. I'd won the affections of a beautiful and popular girl who called our house often. The anger was building up inside of me because I knew the school said I could play and despite my best efforts to change his mind, he started up his power tool back up and told me to go "fetch" more things for him. There was no reason why I shouldn't be able to play other than he was torturing me on purpose. I felt like I'd been punched in the gut. The athletic director was so certain when I hung up the phone I'd be at practice in the morning and if it were a reasonable family I would be at practice. The director assumed he was dealing with a reasonable parent, but I was invisible to my parents and to the school. In my mind, there was no where I could turn for help.

When school started there would be no jersey for me to wear but plenty of poison ivy from working in the field cleaning up his mess. Not too long after school started the girlfriend moved on to greener pastures. The athletic director and guidance counselor both tracked me down in the hallway and offered to call my father. They couldn't understand why my father wouldn't let me play, and I knew if they called him he would blow up on me so I told them I really didn't want to play. They were disappointed and told me maybe next year I could play.

Seeing how right and normal my life should've been and watching it vanish like a mirage was too much for me to watch. My depressed mind exploded like a pressure cooker within a month of school starting. I should've been playing football and enjoying the company of a pretty girl to a movie on a Saturday Night. When I left my home for a week my mind felt dizzy as a result of the tension draining away from me. I saw how other people lived for the first time, and I was in shock at the world I called home.

With the toxic depression and despair eroding me from the inside out, I went back to my drug of choice. I was tired of hurting all the time and I wanted out of it. There was very little he could do or take away from me at that point. He did threaten to take the bible study away from me and the police explorers. I hated the sight of the Junior Varsity Team in the hallway and knew I should've been with them.

I remembered how the gun against my body made me feel. It made me angry he' been calling me sissy all of my life and I hated feeling like a nervous animal trapped in a fenced enclosure pacing back and forth. The summer was over. I had nine months before the start of the next summer. There wasn't going to be another summer like the one I just endured and I was tired of it all. I made a commitment to end it all before the end of the school year to avoid another summer. When I made that choice I felt alive. The adrenalin started to course through me, and I wasn't a sissy anymore. I felt a peace in my mind knowing I was going to a place where no one could hurt me anymore.

Giving up on my future had consequences and subtle signs began to show up in my life that something was seriously wrong. Since I was going to be dead by the end of the school year I had no need of school anymore. Classes I normally carried a passing grade in started to sharply drop off. My will to live argued back with me because when the high from the adrenalin wore off, I fell into a deeper despair. While the world was going on around me, my fight or flight mechanism was trying to argue with me to get help. I reminded it was no good because the school didn't understand my father and my father would never believe the school saying I was suicidal. It was an up and down life and death struggle from the start of the school year to up to the holiday season marking the start of a new year. My addiction to suicidal ideations became the driving force in my life. I wanted out of the muck and mire of life, and into the Promised Land suicide promised me.

My will to live was still very much in charge, and it wasn't going to let me go into the Promised Land without a fight. It wasn't buying what suicide was telling me. My will to live made me test society's response. I made a contract with my will to live. If by crying out to the world somebody saw then I'd take the help. If no one saw, then I gave myself permission to enter the Promised Land. My will to live, with some reluctance, agreed to the contract because based on my past experience, I was invisible to the world and the deck was stacked in favor of suicide. My will to live thought it was worth the agreement because if it fought hard enough and someone noticed then it may bring about the change I desperately needed. My will to live still held on to a glimmer of hope someone would help me.

I looked up suicide in an encyclopedia, found an eerie picture, and spent many hours gazing at the drama captured. The picture was set in the 1960s and it showed a young man perhaps no older than twenty five standing on the ledge of a high-rise building. The police were leaning outside from a next door window trying to coax him to come towards them. What struck me was the difference between the man on the ledge and the officers' faces. The man perched inches from certain death was calm and relaxed while the officers were under a tremendous amount of stress trying to fight for this man's life. The further I moved down the path towards what I thought was going to be my release from it all, the calmer I became.

When the leaves started to fall from the trees, I was still honoring the life contract between suicide and my will to live. I read through the encyclopedia further and saw what signs and symptoms a person considering suicide demonstrated. I gave comic books away and a few other collectables to friends in school and on the bus. I made comments in class about not being around to graduate or a future without me. No one asked me if I was ok, and this served to convince me I wasn't going to be missed. I started to spend a great deal of time wandering the woods near our home. My routine had changed because I wasn't one to just wander through the woods. My will to live was starting to feel uncomfortable with the way things were going, so it changed its tactic the closer I got to the end of the year. It made me consider the gravity of what I was actually considering. I was afraid to shoot myself and wanted to consider other options. I started to carry out dry-runs or rehearsals for the actual suicide to get an idea of what to expect. I hoped in my mind these so called dry runs would draw attention to myself or help prepare me for the final move towards death. I started to cut on myself with sharp objects hoping it would get someone's attention. I left my arms open for the world to see. I became reckless and was involved in minor accidents from falling out of a tree and into a pond all in an effort to test the response of society around me.

By the time the holiday season of 1985, I believed my situation was hopeless. None of my cries for help had been acknowledged and soon it would be the New Year. I intended to honor the contract I had made and it seemed like suicide had won. I wasn't going to endure another summer. No more dry- runs in an effort to draw attention to myself and so I came up with a plan. I decided to smuggle a small rifle out of the house and go into the woods where no one could see or hear. It'd be over quick because I'd aim at my heart and I'd wake up in the Promised Land suicide had been showing me for the last seven months.

My father raised the white flag every year between Thanksgiving and New Year's Day. He no longer yelled at me during holidays and many times lifted the different punishments he doled out prior to the holiday season. For Christmas that year, I got a clock radio and a nice light blue down filled parka. It was warm and it felt like I was wearing a sleeping bag. I'd made up my mind the storm was over. My mind was at peace with my plan laid in place. All I had to do was look for a departure date.

LAST DAY

With the holiday season over and the New Year started, the war zone in our home returned and the clock started to tick. The plan was to follow through with the shooting between New Year's Day and Memorial Day. I didn't know fate would test my resolve so early on. Since I decided I'd be gone before the end of the school year my grade point average collapsed during the semester. On January 23, 1986, I brought home the worst report card of my scholastic career because I didn't care anymore. I knew I'd be in trouble and most likely get hit, have things thrown at me or perhaps the *idiot list* would be brought out again. Nothing prepared me for what was about to happen that night.

My brother was rarely shown the same treatment I was. It may have been because his mother was around to run interference on his behalf. His grades had taken a slight down turn that semester but not the train wreck I had in my pants pocket that evening. My step-mother had gotten home from work before my father, and this is when fate played its hand. My-step mother asked to see my brother's report cards before mine. As she sat at the kitchen table, her look of concern was evident, and my brother started to tremble and whimper from anxiety. The look in his eyes said it all. He knew a storm was coming for him. Experience had taught him how bad the storms could be, and they always hit after dinner. Not only was my brother afraid, but my step- mother was fearful as well on his behalf. As she sat down to comfort him, I stood alone. As she comforted him she looked up at me with fear and said these words to me unknowingly turning the missile keys releasing my suicide plan: *"For your sake, I hope your grades are better than his because I wouldn't put it past your father to hurt you."*

My legs buckled because at that point, it confirmed my deepest hurt and fear. No one sheltered me from his temper like she was doing for my brother. My mother had left long ago and had no contact other than a casual noncommittal note inviting me for a visit. For years, I'd lived with the threat of suffering significant bodily harm at the hand of my father, and my step- mother had seen enough to warn me of this threat that night: *I was in danger of bodily harm by my own father, and it was time for me to go.*

My father had told me, "I'll either make you or break you boy." He never stopped to consider what the consequences were if he actually broke my life. I was surprised at how peaceful I was with the go ahead I'd just given myself. I imagined I was just checking in at a grand airport soon to embark on an airplane that would leave this world and deliver me to a safer place. I was going on a journey. I wanted one night of peace so I set fire to the ships and made it so there would be no turning around should I wake up in the morning and have a change in heart. Without hesitation, I looked at her and ignored the report cards in my pocket. I told her I would have my report cards on Monday and they were some of the best grades I'd ever earned. She thought it was odd I didn't have report cards as well to bring home and was shocked at my sudden improvement in school. *If I was going to do this then I needed to charge right into the mouth of the monster.* If I was going to tell a lie, it was going to be a spectacular lie. I was digging my hole deeper on purpose and there was no coming back from all of the lies I started telling in an effort to keep my hand steady on the wheel as I drove towards the abyss. If I were still there on Monday, I risked having "my teeth knocked out" for lying to my father

My step-mother was relieved at this unexpected surprise because if my grades were an improvement, it may be enough to slow my father's aggression enough so it didn't boil over into their lives. My father got home shortly after having my conversation with my step-mother. He walked past me for a moment, and I felt like I was standing at a check point with forged documents trying to escape from a militarized police state in a free neutral sovereign nation. I felt like he was the border police going through my things. He eyed me up as I tried to act relaxed knowing my report cards were folded up in my pocket. It was too late to come clean because I just lied to my step-mother about having a really strong marking period. He started to ask me questions like he didn't believe my story. I held my ground because the suicide told me freedom was just across the border.

If he believed my lie, it didn't matter because when he finally got my report cards no one could read them because they would be saturated with blood. Fate wasn't finished forcing my hand that night because before I went to sleep he handed me another list to do before he got home from work.

One of the most striking things I remember about January 24, 1986 was how the world appeared. Colors were more vibrant and the sounds of lockers crashing in the school hallway created a terrible clamor in my ears. The air had a heavy and sweet smell about it and it laid across my skin like a blanket. Muscles were tense and as a result of the prolonged body tension at the end of the day, it felt like I had a fever. My fight or flight response mechanism was confused that day; it knew danger was coming and it was working at a heightened level maximizing all of the senses to gather information. *The problem was, I was a mortal threat to myself, and my fight or flight didn't know how to protect me from that.*

As a result of that day I know how the condemned to die on death row feel as they go about their last day on earth.   It was my intention to not live to see Saturday. I boarded the bus for the final trip home and remained silent with my gaze locked onto the world outside of the bus window. With each revolution of the bus tire, I started to feel more apprehensive and I'd wished I could take a nap and pretend for just a moment I was not in this position. If I took a nap then I could just wake up at my house and without any thought get off the bus and carry it out. But if I slept then I'd miss the surrounding beauty I took for granted through my life. I didn't want to miss a tree, bird, horse or cloud. Deep down I knew I didn't want to see this through, but there wasn't any other way out of it but through the door suicide showed me.

When the bus pulled up in front of my bus stop, I mechanically stood up and marched to the bus door. The bus driver told me to have a good weekend. With that comment, I got off the bus and watched it drive away. It was time.

I marched into the house, went directly into my bedroom, and closed the door. I initiated my premade plan as if I were a prisoner about to head over the wire in the middle of the night. From this moment on my actions were mechanical and without emotions until I needed a drink of water and went into the bathroom. As I stood at the vanity I studied my face in the mirror and realized a dead person was looking back at me. I swore at myself for letting that moment of humanity find its way past what I was trying to push through. I went back into my room and wrote out a meaningless suicide note to make them feel better. I felt like I owed it to them. One more time I went back through the house and went into the study where the guns were kept. It started the previous summer when I first heard what suicide promised me, and I was about to find out if those promises were true or not. I pulled out the rifle and bullet and rolled it up in my blue parka and snuck back through the house. My younger brother never looked up from his cartoons so no one knew what I was preparing to do. I put on my best clothes. I put on a shirt, tie and dress shoes. I wanted to look decent when they found me. *My defense mechanism was screaming in my face what I was doing was morally wrong*. It was down in the trench pleading, to "**stop,**" so it changed its strategy and went for my dignity. It wanted me to know this wasn't a dignified thing for me to do and it wanted me to feel shame. Suicide told me to put my best shirt and tie on and get on with it.

With my shirt and tie on I opened the window and slid the rifle out. At this point I no longer felt like I was an active participant in my life and it felt like I was at the back of a movie theater while my life played out across a screen. As I started to climb through the window, my will to live saw a parachute and demanded it come with me. I paused long enough for me to grab my Bible and then I climbed out of the window.

THE BEAST

Over the years I've been asked more times than I can count, *"Why, did you shoot yourself?"* From the second chapter up until this point I've made an attempt to answer why I shot myself on Friday, January 24, 1986. I'd been abandoned by my one parent and treated like an animal by the other. I believed I was invisible to the world. I was exhausted from living in fear and lacked the smallest seed of hope life would ever get any better. I was so intoxicated from suicidal thoughts the actual killing process was marginalized to the point it was nothing more than a minor formality I had to go through to reach the Promised Land. The Promised Land was a peaceful releasing of my spirit from this world to go where no one could hurt me again. Never having been exposed to the level of violence necessary to end life, I was ill prepared to go through the furnace I just plunged into. When the blast hit my body it sobered my mind from the subversive suicidal ideations that sought to destroy my life. No longer under the control of their puppet master like influence I wanted to live; however, my fear was, it was too late.

For every lie there's an opposing truth. When asked, *"Name a reason to live"* ultimately I was asked to find a reason to hope. I was dying but Hope reached down in the midst of the storm and grabbed my hand securely. Suicide told me I was alone, worthless, and pointless to go on. It told me I should focus on releasing and escaping my life because my life it wasn't worth living. Hope said to me, "My life is a gift." I wasn't alone and God was with me if I reached out to Him. My life has a destiny and a purpose. Suicide sought to kill and destroy, but Hope sought to seek and to save what was lost. Suicide left me with scars and nightmares. When the ambulance crew delivered me at the door of the hospital, I knew the next few moments would decide the rest of my life. As they wheeled my stretcher into the trauma room it was Hope's face looking into my eyes reminding me I wasn't alone. When they picked me up off the cot and laid me out on the trauma table, the last thing I saw before I began my descent into the valley of the shadow of death was Hope reaching out to carry me through that shadow. Once I turned my eyes to the One true Hope, He never abandoned me at my darkest hour.

When they moved me onto the trauma table, I'd been hemorrhaging for well over an hour. The total response time from the ambulance station to the scene and from there to the hospital was approximately forty minutes. I'll never know how long I lay in the woods, or how long I lay in the field crying out for help. My conscious state was depleted by the time the hospital staff turned on their examination lights to evaluate the damage done. It seemed like the activity in the trauma room was going on in another dimension and not in my personal space. There were times when the bright exam lights would disappear, and I'd find myself in a quiet restful state. From another time and space, I heard a member of the trauma team warn others to hold me still because of what they were preparing to do. Their exact words were, **_"this is going to hurt."_** The shooting was a hell on its own but the chest tube insertion took the moment to another level. When they pushed the end of the chest tube catheter into my side, I left the peaceful place I'd retreated to and found myself once more part of a violent reality suicide never showed me as the doctors fought to save my life.

At one point in the chaotic trauma room, I woke up slightly, pivoted my head to the right and saw my family outside of the trauma room looking in at me. I was so glad to see them and wanted them to know I was fine. My family covered their faces in grief and walked away from the trauma room. I wanted to yell for them to come back and not leave me. They'd left me, and I was sad they'd walked away and very concerned they'd expressed such an outpouring of grief when I knew I was fine.

I have memory fragments, but they belong to someone else. These fragments don't make sense and there is no basis in experience. There is the sensation of someone touching my heart. There is a recurring thought, _"The hands are working to keep me on the table. They are_ *doing more violence to my chest than the gun did, and it's no longer necessary. I'm fine."* At some point in time my consciousness *knew I wasn't going to die* from the gunshot wound before *I can remember what space I was occupying. I am overjoyed I am not going to die by my own hand.* **Then I woke up in the intensive care unit.**

When I woke up in the Intensive Care Unit on Sunday, January, 26, 1986, I felt *"different"*. I went into the woods on January 24th with one perception of reality and when I regained a conscious state on the 26th my perception of reality had been altered. It felt like I lived in a house that had a window facing the eastern horizon and one day I decided to go for a trip and I left my house empty for a season. While I was gone a carpenter came into the house and moved the window from the eastern horizon and created a new window so it faced the north east horizon. The change was a subtle change but enough of a change so that I could tell I was looking at the world from a different window.

On Tuesday, January 28th, 1986, four days after my shooting, was been moved to a general medical floor to continue my recovery. My head was foggy, and I struggled to manage a foam cup of ice shavings. At 11:38 AM EST, the Space Shuttle Challenger disaster unfolded on live television. As I watched the shuttle disintegrate across the sky, a foreign thought entered my mind: *"They went further than me."* No one from the hospital staff had pulled up a stool next to my bed to chat about the other night. I was alone in my hospital room watching in real time the space shuttle break apart, and as it broke apart, I knew I'd shared an understanding with them as they went through the *veil* onto the other side. In my heart I knew I'd touched the *veil* as well, but instead of going through like they had I was held and sent back. I wasn't permitted to go through all the way because the hands held me from going, and my prayer had been answered. When I said, *"/send an Angel to deliver me from this moment."* I asked God to deliver my life.

When I went to visit the surgeon in his office for my follow up care he wanted me to know I was very fortunate to be alive. He told me *"The only reason why you're alive today is because of how healthy and strong you were before the shooting. It seems all of that exercise saved your life."* I've had doctors look at the bullet scar and say, *"That's a hard one to come back from."* Many times my family told me, *"You came real close to being gone forever."*

Discussing my near fatal experience has always been the most difficult thing for me to face because I never wanted to know how far things went that night. The mere suggestion that I may have died by my own hand even for a brief moment or even the lights inside of me flickered for a moment was deeply disturbing to me. When I was under the influence of suicide's lie, I never actually considered it killing myself because the end justified the means. All I focused on was the goal and the goal was to be released from this body. The mere suggestion I may have succeeded in taking my life based on a lie, and the only reason why I survived my suicide was through a direct intervention beyond the human realm was unsettling. It was troublesome because of the enormity of what I'd unleashed into my life, and I owed a debt of gratitude. My will to live was a high fence set around my life to protect me, and Suicide's promises offered me a hand up and over that fence. As I was crossing over the fence and saw what was waiting for me on the other side, I regretted ever touching the fence.

The few memories I have resemble pages from a flip book. When I lay out the memory fragments in chronological order, put them into my flip book, and slowly flip the pages the story starts to unfold. The once still fragments take on a life of their own, and I can see the staff wheel my near unresponsive body into the trauma room. With each page passing before my eyes, I see more details never noticed before. When I reach the end of the book, I start back over from the beginning. This time I flip the pages faster and again I reach the end of those memories in chronological order. Starting from the beginning at an even faster pace I pass over the book and more details surface until I see something that takes my breath away.

Prior to writing this book, I never considered I lost my life that day. I didn't want to know, but in order to heal, I needed to face all of it and address it accordingly. My medical records are long gone, and no ever came out and told me directly because many times I'd avoid the conversation. I have no memories or experiences of what some have described as a typical near-death experience. I never saw ladders, tunnels or the only bright light I saw came from the overhead exam light just above me. I have no recollections of hovering above myself as the doctors worked to save me. It wasn't until I made my imaginary flip book that I saw one detail leap out at me from the picture. The memory in question involves my family looking in at me as I lay in the trauma room. I can see they are overwhelmed with grief, and I'm concerned for their welfare and wanted to tell them I was fine. Over the years, they told me at that moment when they saw me they thought I was "gone". I argued with them I saw them and I was fine. Many times they looked at me with a puzzled expression.

As the flip book buzzed through my fingers the detail that came at me was how *fine* I felt. I was physically empty when they moved my body onto the trauma table, but suddenly I felt a reprieve from my fading condition as I looked up at my family. It wasn't like when I went unconscious, when I had a moment to rest from the crushing sensation in my chest I'd been battling for almost two hours. Also, a fair amount of time had passed after the shooting so I imagine my airway was protected by having my head in line with my spine. I was able to pivot my head and make eye contact with them I wanting them to know I was fine. They didn't see me looking at them from a space of about twenty feet, and they turned their back on me and walked away under the impression I was dead. When I saw these details take a life of their own, I felt like I was a parked car at the bottom of a steep hill and runaway dumpster had just slammed into the side of me.

I wanted to run away from this flip book and what I saw: *my family walking away from a dead child in a trauma room, memory fragments with no basis for the experience, the space shuttle crew, and comments from doctors over the years and feeling different when I woke up.* The evidence dropped at my feet with the weight of a hundred metropolitan city phone directories. **I died; I actually killed myself with a rifle.** I felt a door inside of me open up. It wasn't a typical front door found on the front of a residential home built to keep intruders out. This door was built from steel forged in a foundry fire to resist the heaviest of siege laying armies, but its purpose wasn't to keep an intruder out. It was laid in place to keep something in. I could hear the door unlock with a loud clunk, and its heavy hinges moaned under the weight of the heavy door as it swung open very slowly. Something slowly stepped out from behind the door and stretched its body to look at me. It was the beast. It was the beast I'd not seen in over ten years, the beast that I saw when I fell over the fence that night. *I actually succeeded in taking my life and had it not been for God, I would not have been given the second chance.* The beast let out a familiar roar as it stepped toward the core of my life.

I could see myself walking into the woods once more with the rifle. I could taste the gunpowder in my mouth and feel the bolt action working in my hands. Again, I saw the dreaded metal light coming for me. The metal light always cloaks the bullet just prior to it hitting me square in the chest. I was in the middle of this book when I had to go to the hospital for an evaluation for severe Post- Traumatic Stress Disorder symptoms. They were the most severe symptoms I have experienced since my late twenties. It was time for the beast to come out from that door so I could face it and not be afraid of it anymore. "When an Angel Intervenes" was a key to unlock the door that kept the beast behind the door. I've started regular counseling to help with the untreated depression I have lived with most of my life along with the symptoms associated with Post- Traumatic Stress Disorder. If I passed through the veil or only touched it, it doesn't really matter. From the moment I knew I wasn't going to do die from suicide, I was very grateful for another chance to live my life. I wanted to jump up and tell the world about my experience and what God had delivered my life from. I'd asked Him to deliver me from the death and He did. I'd been in the jaws of a beast but its grasp was released from my body. It was a beast suicide had hid from me. I never really wanted to die. I had every intention of dying but what I really wanted was life change. I could no longer accept the terms life was dealing me. Suicidal ideations made what seemed like an attractive offer of escape, peace and release from it all. When the energy from the end of the gun exploded into my life, it was more powerful than suicides lie, and it broke its spell it had me under. Suicide didn't care it brought yet another life to that point. It left me on my own and it had finished with me.

I wasn't allowed to celebrate it didn't kill me and I wanted to savor my new extension on life. However, it was time to cover my face with the cloak of shame and hide. As far as many were concerned, there was nothing for me to celebrate about, *"You actually tried to kill yourself."*

THE VILLAGE

My enthusiasm for life was quickly tempered when my family told me, *"It would've been better for you to have lost your legs in an accident or been burned in a fire because people can see and understand those scars, but these scars no one will understand."* At any moment, I was afraid the police would come arrest me for trying to murder myself. The people in and outside of my hospital room were whispering about what I'd done to myself. My family and medical community were very concerned about how the public would receive me, and they told me I needed to create a story about how I was shot. I hadn't started shaving yet and I narrowly missed dying by a self-inflicted gun-shot wound by a margin of an inch and a few minutes. However, following a discussion with my surgeon and going over the details about my surgery, I soon discovered the margin between life and death wasn't as wide as I first thought.

My body and spirit hummed like a tuning fork. I looked in a mirror on the bedside tray at the image of my face. The face I saw in the mirror was not the same face I saw looking back from the bathroom vanity an hour before I shot myself. There was no life in those eyes. Though this face was covered with cuts and abrasions, I did see life looking back at me. Though it was pale, gaunt, battered and bruised, it was alive. They told me my face had been battered as a result of it being dragged through the woods. Under my hospital gown I could see tubes carrying bloody drainage to a collection port on the floor. I gently probed the left side of my upper body but I couldn't feel exactly where my fingers were touching. The only thing I felt were my fingers touching metal staples across the front of my chest. A kind nursing assistant came in one morning to help me bathe and freshen up. He filled up a plastic tub with tepid water and started to unsnap the hospital gown.

After he helped me remove the gown, I was able to see the scars the beast had left behind.

When I left for school on the 24th of January, there wasn't a scratch on my body but by the end of the day, it had been changed forever. I saw scars everywhere, and from what the scars were telling me a desperate battle had been waged to save my life. I saw chest tube drains leaving just above my waistline. The nursing assistant took a mirror to show me the *surgical scar.* The thoracotomy scar went from my left pectoral muscle and from what I could see in the mirror it stopped an inch from my spine, and it was over a half inch wide. The nursing assistant whistled and said, *"Boy, they cut you in half, what'd you do to yourself?"* It was the first time I ever had to admit to any one I actually shot myself on purpose. From what I could see the surgeon had to lay me on my side and carve half way across the thickness of my body to alter the damage I'd done to myself. I could see the metal staples. Until they were removed, I was afraid they were the only thing holding me together, and if I coughed wrong, I risked having my heart fall out of my chest. My chest felt like an egg cracked open on the side of a skillet and then it had been glued back together. A nurse came in to help the nursing assistant because the time had come for them to change the bandage over the bullet scar, and the surgeon was due in to see me. The nurse gently pulled back on the bandage though I couldn't feel the tape pulling at my skin. The nurse told me the wound was healing nicely because it was pink and there were no signs of infection. The nurse and I weren't looking at the same wound because from what I saw the wound looked charred and blackened from the molten steel that passed through me with relative ease.

The surgeon came to see me on his rounds, and as he flipped through my chart he looked down at me. What he told me sent a powerful shockwave through me, and it was enough to send me back in time by a few days. The surgeon explained to me he'd left a bullet fragment behind due to its proximity to my spine. It was too close and not worth the risk in removing it. As the surgeon spoke, I wasn't listening anymore because I found myself sitting on that crate again in front of the tree and not in my hospital room. When he asked me if there were any further questions, I saw the brilliant muzzle flash once more as I experienced my first Post-Traumatic Stress Disorder Flashback. As I experienced the flashback, I wanted to scream for it to stop because it was so realistic I knew what was behind the muzzle flash, and it was coming for me again. Sadly, as I've gone through life I've been shot more than once, and it was another truth suicide hid from me. A failed suicide attempt often leaves life lasting scars that can range anywhere from social stigma to permanent brain damage. After the surgeon left my room, I knew what happened after the bullet hit me. The bullet broke into fragments some of it missed my heart by an inch and one of the fragments came to a rest near my spinal cord. The surgeon left the fragment next to the spine alone because based on his expertise there was a greater risk in removing it. If a skilled surgeon didn't feel comfortable operating so close to my spinal cord without paralyzing me, then how did I miss damaging it with a piece of metal moving close to 1500 feet per second? My chest had turned into a tin can, someone tossed a few small rocks and gave it a good shake because this is what happened when the bullet hit. The window of survivability had been drastically reduced, and my life spared as I felt bullet fragments bounce around me while an invisible hand protected my spinal cord. If the fragment had severed the spinal cord, then I'd never been able to move towards help and surely would've lost my life where my body hit the ground.

When the medical staff left me alone to my thoughts, I imagined my shattered body was held together with staples. On the inside I could feel the metal buzzing near my spine like an angry bee hive. I was struggling to create a story how I'd been shot while I nervously kept checking the door wondering how much longer before the police came looking for me. The bullet scar pulsed in rhythm with my heart screaming, *"Shame!"* each time it took another life giving beat. Nurses, doctors, family all whispered just out of ear shot on the other side of the room or out in the hallway. Occasionally a whisper would float into my ear and I'd hear, *"He actually tried to kill himself? Why?"* I was told a person burned severely in a fire stood a better chance with public perception than I did because those scars were visible and my scars were hidden. The burn victim didn't get their scars from suicide unlike mine. Both the burn victim and I'd survived a traumatic event but mine was a result of an intentional act through suicide. When people came to visit, I could see the bewildered looks on their faces. I wanted to ask them to not look at me like that. My scars meant I wanted to live. I believed a lie, and it promised to deliver my life but it was too late. I had pulled the trigger, the bullet wasn't ever going to come back, and there would be no compassion shown to me.

The center of my chest was invisible to touch and this numb invisibility made me feel like I had a gaping hole in the middle of me. I wasn't a boy anymore given the pardon of all pardons and a second chance to live my life. My battle with the beast had turned me into a *reanimated monster* that needed to keep out of sight of the village for the rest of my life. If my fictitious story weren't believable enough, then villagers would hunt me down with ropes and torches because they were afraid of what they didn't understand and they were already asking me, "why?" and I hadn't been discharged from the hospital yet.

The day of my discharge, there was an awkward encounter in my room between the surgeon and my family. When I was lying in the field and not sure if I were going to survive I made a solemn vow to never do this again. I realized life was a gift, and I hated that I quit on my own gift. My family wanted me to carve it in stone for them I'd never do this again, and I assured them it would never happen again. The nurses and social workers told my family since I'd attempted suicide in the past then there was a high probability I'd try again and possibly succeed in the future. What I tried to tell them was, I'd already succeeded on my first attempt. The only reason why I survived was due to an intervention, and I'd come as close as anyone could ever get to death from suicide and returned after touching the veil. My suicide wasn't a carefully crafted daredevil, death defying *"cry for help."* I set out that day to die in the woods. I saw something after I pulled the trigger making me realize I'd been lied to and I wanted to live. ***I chose to move towards help because I wanted to live!*** I was about to learn my first lesson about life inside of the village. I had fallen under the spell of the beast before and since I'd fallen, I could never be trusted again. As far as the village was concerned I was weak and broken because I tried to kill myself.

I had my family convinced it would never happen again when the surgeon came through the door to see me off. He wanted me to see a psychiatrist, but my family resisted him. They told him I was fine and promised to never *"do a stunt like that again."* The village was already having a difficult time with me. As life would move along, I would find there were certain rules to live under while you lived in the village. What I discovered about the village was they didn't feel comfortable with anyone that had to see a *"shrink"* or a *"head doctor"*, and I needed one. They were already lighting the torches because I needed the help of a psychiatrist.

Though I'd been discharged from the hospital, I found the beast still lurking in the shadows and angry with me because at the last moment I reached out for Hope and not **it**. It had me in its grasp, and I slipped through its claws. I found the beast had the ability to change shapes to blend in with its new reality. The beast knew I wanted to live and because I knew its nature, I'd been immunized against its poison. It changed its shape to fit my new life and it wouldn't go away quietly or without a fight. It figured since it didn't take my life that day, it would try and rob me of my *quality of life.* The beast transformed itself into individual toxic nuclear fuel rods. In order for my life to move on, I needed a way to live with the poison of those toxic memories. Like a nuclear reactor and its cooling pond, that's what I built in my own life. Unknowingly, my highest purpose in life was about managing and protecting my life from the damaging effects of memories from the shooting and my battle with suicide. I shoved the memories deep into my core and submerged them under chilled water devoting a large portion of my life's energy to monitoring the condition of the cooling pond to prevent a meltdown. The beast still had its grip on my life through Post Traumatic Stress Disorder.

It wouldn't take long for me to understand what this new reality meant for my life. When I got home from the hospital I'd lost a considerable amount of weight. I was tired, weak and in pain. However, when I tried to retreat to the world of sleep and rest the shooting played across the screen of my dreams. There were no pleasant dreams to carry me away for a night of rest and healing. When I tried to close my eyes, I saw the end of a gun once more against my chest. Once more, eyes flashed in horror at the site of the muzzle flash and I could taste the bitter gunpowder. The air was always sweet from blood washing over me like it did that day. Each night when I went to sleep this is what I saw and it robbed me of rest. Every night when I went to bed, I could see from my bedroom window the woods where I narrowly escaped, and it felt like eyes were watching and staring at me. Unable to get the needed rest, I started to feel the protective coolant slosh around inside of me. The reactor was already heating up.

Overcome with a new form of anxiety, it seemed to have an air of death and violence in it. The anxiety I used to feel when I had to face my father's temper was nothing more than the pre-game warm-up compared to this. When this anxiety hit me, it felt like a bullet was ripping through me. I would instinctively jump and try and protect myself from something that wasn't there. Instead of worrying about how my father may respond to bad grades, I was trying to run the sensation of the guns bolt action out of my hands. No one knew about the beast's new strategy and couldn't protect me from its savage attacks against my mind and body.

I'd been given a new radio as a get well gift. One night while I was struggling to fall asleep, I turned on the radio and spun the dial. I hadn't enjoyed a full nights rest since I got home, and my body was worn out from everything. I came across a Christian radio station and turned the volume down so it was barely audible. I never knew the content of those broadcast. I only knew it was a radio preacher teaching from his bible. Along with biblical teaching, they honored God with praise and worship music. I discovered I was able to fall asleep feeling safe and secure with this station on all night. My heart and mind felt still and at peace. The water around the memories grew still at the sound of what was coming from the radio. The beast grew still before the words that came before the radio. I didn't feel eyes burning a hole through me from the woods anymore.

During this time I received an unusual phone call. On the other end of the line was the voice of an adult I'd never talked to before. Her voice was cheerful and cautious, but she insisted she had to speak with me. The person on the other end of the line was the mother of the friendly girl who sat behind me in class and frequently shared her faith with me. She had even invited me to her house for Bible studies. She was one of the few friends I had regular contact with. Her mother said to me, "Jimmy, I know you're going to think this is crazy. I was vacuuming my house and out of the air, a voice spoke to me. I know we don't know each other, and you're probably thinking 'who's this crazy lady on the other end of the phone?'" When she told me her vacuuming had been interrupted by a voice I wasn't shocked. I had such a voice reach out to me not too long ago. She went on to tell me how the voice was so intrusive she had to shut her vacuum off and listen for a moment. The voice that spoke with me stated, *"name a reason to live"* wanted me to raise my head up and look beyond my circumstance and hold fast to hope. The voice that spoke to me in the woods saved my life. The voice wasn't finished because now it was sending a messenger to me. The voice led me towards physical life, and now it was leading me towards the Hope of eternal life. The nice lady on the phone asked if she could come and visit me, and I told her it would be fine.

After a few days, she came to my house with her Bible and ice cream. She shared with me the good news of God's love for me. God loved me but my sin nature served as an impassable canyon keeping me from fellowship with Him. *My sin separates me from God.* God wanted to reconcile my life with Him and bring me into a relationship with Him through His son's death on a cross. She told me the story of Jesus' life, death and resurrection. I heard stories of His loving touch on the lives of everyday people like the blind man and countless other hurting and broken people in His day. I also knew the story of Easter and Good Friday and the three men on the crosses of Calvary. One of them was a common thief, and as he hung next to

Jesus nearing the point of death, he asked mercy from Jesus. Jesus in His own physical suffering loved the man more than His own suffering acknowledged this man's desire for life and mercy. I was acquainted with the physical torments of death, and I couldn't imagine acknowledging another person's life in the middle of that storm let alone a thief next to me. I also knew from personal experience the incredible power of death, but even that crushing power couldn't contain Jesus because in three days He rose from the dead.

She shared many Bible verses that day with me and one of them was, Revelation3:20:

> *"Here I am! I stand at the door and knock. If*
> *anyone hears my voice and opens the door,*
> *I will come in and eat with him and he with*
> *Me."*

Here in His word God, wanted a relationship with me because He loved me. He'd been knocking on the door to my life all of these years and all I had to do was open the door. All I had to do was believe it was true, repent of my sin, ask Him to forgive me and come into my life.

I wanted this father-son relationship. A relationship I could climb into my father's lap and feel safe and secure. I knew it was His name I called on just prior to squeezing the trigger, and it was His name I whispered when the bullet hit me. Here, I sat less than two weeks after that moment alive in front of a messenger of God who was sharing the good news of God's love with me. My will to live that day knew when I headed out to take my life I needed a parachute, and it reached for God's word. Though in one hand I carried the instrument to take my life, in the other hand, I carried a love letter to me from God. His love letter, His sacrifice, His hope and delivering on that promise revealed to my life God's love was genuine, and I didn't want this canyon of sin separating my life from Him anymore. I wanted to run across it and offer my life up to him. *I humbled my knee before Him and asked that He would forgive me of my sin and would He please come into my life and be the Lord of it!*

The stillness in my heart kept the coolant level at a safe level, and the toxic memories were away from my life. I assumed because God was now my father, He'd open every door I wanted Him to whenever I wanted Him to do so. My family took me to see the psychiatrist a couple a times a week at first. At the first appointment, I sat out in the hallway by myself as my family and psychiatrist discussed my life. Through the thin office wall I could hear more whispers and murmurs about my life and what I'd done to myself. My father was ashamed I was seeing the psychiatrist and told me when I turned 18 this time in my life would be sealed shut and no one would ever know about it. I had to lie about how I was shot and now I had to hide I needed a *"shrink"*. My apprehension about society and their opinion about my life grew daily. After the initial consultation, I was on my own despite the doctor's desire my family attend with me. They were of the opinion this was a formality because I agreed to never try to kill myself again. Since I promised to never shoot myself again, then I was all better inside. The only support I received in trying to put the pieces of my life back together following my *"botched suicide attempt"* was the twice a week visit to the psychiatrist that were reduced to one time per week for one hour. My family didn't have a faith in God and told me they didn't believe so there wasn't a church for me to go and find support and fellowship with other believers. I did have access to a few believers at school and an occasional bible study or a Christian based athletic fellowship. So I held church in my room every day after school. I tuned in and turned up the Christian radio station I found and followed along in my bible with the different radio broadcasts. When they played music, I would sing along in worship and reverence towards God who restored my life.

During my time with the doctor, he wanted me to free write. He knew the free writing would draw things out from my subconscious mind. I'd told him everything I knew: My suicide planning, my final day, the internal struggle to pull the trigger and the moments after the gun went off. He wasn't satisfied and felt my subconscious mind was blocking things from him that may help in my recovery. This bothered me over the years because I never revealed anything to him that I personally wasn't aware of. But I do remember my family meeting with him in private, and the many conversations through life how close I came to dying from suicide. Did the doctor know my subconscious mind saw something that day and it was protecting me from what it saw and refused to give it up until I was ready to see? On the paper he wanted me to just write out whatever came to my mind. He encouraged me to think about that day and create a story. Let the creative subconscious mind weave a story together and stay out of its way to see what turns up, much like I did when I wrote "When an Angel Intervenes". "When Angel Intervenes" was the key to unlock the window to see what my subconscious mind was hiding from me. I had arrived at the point in my life where my mind felt it was safe enough to let it out. Two months after I opened the window, the reactor and beast blew apart into my life.

The issues why I shot myself were never addressed during this time. I was told I shot myself over normal teen issues, or it was nothing more than an extravagant cry for help. I was feeling defeated already, and it hadn't been a full year since my shooting. I had to lie to people how I was shot. My body had been ravaged with ugly scars, and since I couldn't escape my own body, there would be no escaping my suicidal past. To add insult to my body perception, it hurt most days and I couldn't feel or see the center of my chest. My own body was serving as a trigger to those toxic memory rods I was trying to keep stored away. Whenever I looked down at my chest I could see the bullet hole puling in rhythm to my heart, and it shook me to my foundation. I felt so guilty for shooting myself I used to lay down on my back with no shirt on and purposely watch it beat. Most of my upper body still hadn't regained the sense of touch further adding to this feeling; I had a gaping hole in the middle of me. I also had to hide in shame I was under the care of a psychiatrist, and if anyone knew my "secret" then it was presumed I wasn't able to manage the affairs of my life without trying to kill myself.

I felt like I'd been punched in the gut when people said, "It's a cry for help." It was presumed at the time; I woke up one day and decided to shoot myself in an effort to draw attention to myself. I was a disturbed young man with a deep mental illness with nothing better to do then put a hole in the center of his chest. No one really knew I'd tried to reach out for seven months. My family was busy avoiding the psychiatrist and telling me to hide it all. No one knew of my total frustration when I tried to bring the school and my family together on the matter of me playing football. If a line of communication couldn't be established on that simple issue, then no one would believe me when I knew I was in over my head. No one asked me what it was like to sit for days confined to a steel chair. I hauled hundreds of piles of brush for days, months and years with almost no chance to be a kid. The ones that only saw that I shot myself didn't know how I felt about being compelled to refer to one person as "Mom" while the one I actually knew as Mom wrote my life off. People often stared at me as if they may catch my suicide. Those people weren't around when I felt like my home was littered in egg shells and I was afraid at any time I would step on one. Cracking egg shells never ended well for me because many times it unleashed a torrent of destructive abuse much like the day I had to duck my head to avoid a chainsaw coming at it.

The ones who wanted to cast a stone at me for seeking to escape my life through suicide where not there when I had to wipe blood from my lip and told it was my fault. I was told it was my fault because, *"You got me pissed off at you, and I lost my temper."* What the village saw was suicide and not a person. They didn't see a human in need of compassion, grace and an ear to listen because what he did was too far beyond the scope of humanity and unworthy of such a healing sentiment. The village monster was in fear of his life and sought refuge in the caves away from them. In the end, I didn't owe society an apology like I thought I did. The person I really needed to forgive was *me* so I could heal from it all.

ONE YEAR ANNIVERSARY

By December 1986, I started to feel an uneasy dread about going through the upcoming month of January. The crisp smell of winter in my nose and the way the sun hung low on the horizon that time of year reminded me of the year prior. The calming relationship I had with God kept the water over the memory rods and away from my life since the previous spring.

However, with the approaching anniversary, the water turned into a rolling boil, and with the evaporating steam, the rods were getting red hot. By the time January 1987 came about, the memories were as vivid as they were the week after the shooting. I could hear the twigs break under my shoes as I walked through the woods though I hadn't stepped into the woods in a year. Though the new coat I wore was brown, when I went to button it: It turned blue like the one I wore the winter before. In the middle of this ghost like blue coat was a small tear in the fabric. A tear created by the bullet I fired a year before.

It was agreed by the adults I wasn't a threat to myself, and it was decided the services of the psychiatrist were no longer needed. Privately I was told, "Own it. You're the one who shot yourself. You're not going to do anything stupid like that anymore, are you?" I knew I wasn't going to try and end my life anymore. Since there wasn't a threat anymore then it was a waste of time to keep seeing the doctor as it was explained to me.

From the time I was released from the hospital, the environment in my home became more relaxed. There was time for recreation and no more time spent wasting away in my prison- cell- like bedroom. My father no longer threw things at me and even apologized once for everything. He let me try out for the Varsity football team that fall. I wasn't able to keep up with the other players, and I was afraid of taking a hit in the ribs so I chose to not play football anymore, but the coach found a place for me as an equipment manager.

I'd put back on most of my weight after the one year anniversary. I still avoided the woods and rarely glanced down in the direction of them. My father still continued on with his normal routine around his property just without me and not at the fevered pace he had since the day he bought the land. I could tell he was growing annoyed with me for staying away from the woods. One pleasant spring weekend in 1987, I had a biology report due and had to collect some bugs. It was the first time I had to go into woods, but I made it work by avoiding the woods I'd shot myself in. I went into our neighbor's woods to collect the necessary specimens, and I was relieved to be done with the exercise. As I walked up the lane towards my home, my father met me halfway home and confronted me. He told me it was time for me to go back into *the woods and go to the spot.* He told me it was time for me to stop being afraid of this, and I needed to own it all. I felt like I couldn't swim as he drove a motor boat out into the ocean and proceeded to kick me off the side and watched me sink knowing I couldn't swim.

He made me walk into the woods and find the tree where I'd sat in front of. I felt a vibration in the ground and my head started to swim when I stood before the tree. There was an energy coming out from the ground, and it felt like it was going to open up and swallow me alive. The temperature inside the reactor started to move towards a dangerous level. I could see inside of me the rods were starting to glow red hot. To my father, it was a warm pleasant spring afternoon, but to me, the air had a winter's bite in it. All around him he saw plush spring foliage, but to me, the woods were dark and void of life. My father was within arm's reach of me and in any normal situation I could've heard his whisper from that distance. From the place I was at, his voice was nothing more than a feint radio signal broadcasting over a weak transmission. Occasionally, his voice would break through the, white noise in garbled words. Though he saw me standing next to him I didn't see him, standing next to me. I was no longer there. I heard him say something about," *having to bite his tongue over the past year and the time had come for him to air his grievances about what I'd done to him"* while standing in front of **the** tree.

I could see his mouth move but I wasn't paying attention because the ground was shaking. What my father didn't know was the tree had unlocked the door and the beast had come back for me. The beast was angry with me for leaving this place, and it was out there somewhere in the woods watching me with its eyes. As he droned on about how *"angry he was with me"*, I heard what sounded like a horse neighing somewhere just out of sight. I could hear it snort and scratch at the earth. I looked around anxious to see where the beast was going to come from. My father didn't know about the beast because he wasn't initiated to the world I'd exposed myself to that day. The beast was mounted on horseback and outfitted in armor and was preparing to ride me down with a broad sword.

I saw the muzzle flash, but this time instead of pausing in time just before it hits like it did in many of the nightmares and flashback in the past, this one enveloped me. Feeling dizzy, I wanted to hold onto something, but I was afraid to reach out and grab the tree because that would have made this episode more severe. I could feel the surgeon crack into me in an effort to stop the internal bleeding. I could hear the sound of armor clinking and what sounded like a sword being pulled from a sheath. I was frantic to leave this place forever and never comeback as I desperately looked to get away from the impending danger. My brain believed I was truly in danger of losing my life because of the past trauma. I could hear the horse and beast rider advance through the woods towards me.

I'd been yanked out of counseling a year after a near successful attempt at taking my own life because it was embarrassing to my family. I saw things on that day that would make a combat veteran consider me a brother born through fire and blood. These memories were locked inside of me, and when they were unlocked, they were so violent and traumatizing they made my brain believe the danger was real. Very few villagers had been initiated into the world of the beast- rider because they've never been exposed to that much terror or danger. My father continued to speak, and I could make out he was saying something about me getting over and getting on with what I'd done here last year. My vision turned crimson as I got blood into my eyes because there was so much of it.

The rider broke out of the woods, and I could see his fierce anger burning into me.

Even in what should have been the safety of my own home, there were villagers with torches and ropes looking to get rid of the reanimated monster and his ugly suicidal past and his need for mental health care. There was no safe place for me to go and get away from what I had done to myself. At every turn in my life, there stood a person with an opinion about my suicide instead of offering a cool glass of water and a compassionate ear to sit and listen. All anyone wanted to know was, *"Are you going to shoot yourself again in the future?"* As I felt my legs buckle under the weight of this violent energy that had been unlocked from my central nervous system, I felt another presence come over me. I knew this presence and it made the beast rider turn and flee. My father stopped lecturing me in front of the tree because he had *"gotten it off his chest."* Though I know the world of the beast, I also became aware of my Heavenly Father's interventions at particular moments in my life. I can feel His hand guiding, protecting or blessing me. Sometimes, I can also feel a stern hand on my life when it needs correction because He corrects those He calls *"child."*

I was an active police explorer and still planned on pursuing my dream of being a police officer when I turned twenty- one. However, at one meeting, I was confronted by a law enforcement official who was aware of my past and they recommended I consider a new career path. No police department would ever hire me because of my suicidal past and as far as they were concerned, I was a liability to a community. There was even some discussion about whether the sheriff's department would want me to stay active as a police explorer. I was crushed at was happening to me. Some of my peers wanted to go on and play college sports, go to medical school, law school, veterinarian school, or study to be a teacher. I wanted to be a cop from the moment I heard one come to my elementary school, and we wrote letters to our local police department thanking them for coming to see us. There was nothing else I wanted to do, and I refused to believe my suicide would keep me from pursuing my child hood dream.

There were two suicides in my school just over a year after my shooting. A member of my schools' faculty and a fellow classmate both died from gunshot wounds. When I heard of their deaths, I knew something no one else in the school did.   I knew what they saw when they pulled the trigger.   As news of their death slammed into my body, I saw the trigger pull followed by the muzzle flash. The muzzle flash rips back the veil to another world they'd been ignorant of just like I'd been at one point. If they'd only known about that world, they probably wouldn't have pulled the trigger like I did. The **shared experience** sensation rolled through my mind like a far off clap of thunder during a sudden pop up thunder shower. I felt a strong sense of guilt each time the two of them died by what I narrowly missed dying from. There was no one for me to really talk to about these feelings. They sent in crisis counselors, but as far as one was concerned, my shooting was accidental so I couldn't share with anyone my survivor's guilt or the shared experience when they ripped back the veil to the other world and met the beast. Though the beast didn't take me, it remained busy taking other lives, and it reminded me to stay away and keep my mouth shut because it killed me once before.

The rest of high school was uneventful. I attended both of my proms, marched in parades, and was permitted to go to movies with friends. I learned to drive and my grades improved. The guidance counselors made my work load lighter and my post-traumatic stress disorder attacks became less frequent. The water was stable in the reactor, and I felt optimistic about my future. I ignored the advice given to me about choosing another career path, and decided I'd join the military post graduation and pursue being a military policeman.

My father told me to not tell the recruiter I'd shot myself. I did well on my written test and did like my father told me and made no mention of the suicide attempt. The recruiter was confident I'd make it in and could serve in the capacity of a military policeman. The recruiter picked me up one morning and drove me to get my physical unaware of my past. At the processing station they took my blood pressure and had me look at eye charts. All day, people in starched white coats poked and prodded me. When it came my turn to sit down with the military doctor he asked me about my thoracotomy scar, and asked how I'd been shot so close to my heart? I can't escape my past because I can't escape my own body so I had to tell him the truth. I assured him I felt fine, and it was ancient history. I'd been given a clean bill of health by the Psychiatrist. He looked at me over his glasses and told me there was no point in going forward because I was finished. He scribbled in my chart and I put my shirt back on and walked back through the other recruits as they waited their turn to see the doctor. Many of them went further down the hall as I went back to the lobby to wait the few hours for the recruiter to pick me up. He assumed I'd pass without any problem and would not need the entire allotted time to go through the health screening. He didn't count on me having a thoracotomy scar with a bullet scar and as soon as the military doctors saw this, they'd pulled me out and said was unfit to serve. So I sat in the lobby of the processing station just outside the doors marked **"Authorized Personnel Only"** with a drink and knew this was as close as I'd ever get to serve my country. The suicidal past had kept me from passing through the door marked **"Authorized Personnel Only."**

A few times after my near fatal suicide attempt, I had the opportunity to attend various youth camps. Many times the last night of the camp there was an open microphone opportunity for the teenagers to get up and share what God had done for them recently. Many times the other teens would get up and share how God help them win a football game, resist peer pressure or find a missing pet. I was so excited to hear how God was active in everyone else's lives, I assumed they'd want to hear what God delivered me from. I took my place at the end of the line and waited my turn to approach the microphone. The crowd laughed and applauded at the different testimonies my fellow campers shared. I was so excited to share with the crowd what Jesus had done for me. My life had been transformed as a result of a prayer I made to God before I pulled the trigger, and it was a miracle I was alive to stand before them and proclaim God's goodness.

The person in front of me finished and the crowd clapped for the camper. They passed me on the stage as I approached the microphone. As I stood in front of hundreds of other teenagers, the room was silent as they waited for me to tell them about my encounter with God. I opened my mouth and out came the testimony and events surrounding January 24th 1986. I told them how thankful I was to God for His restorative power and how He walked with me through the valley of death but I wasn't afraid because I knew He was with me. I went on for a few more minutes. As I spoke I could feel the power of God flow through my body because I knew what He'd done for my life. The electricity came from me and went out into hundreds of teenagers. The testimony rocked them.   They sat still for minutes and not a word was spoken. I could hear a mouse rustling through a box of cereal in the back kitchen. Feeling awkward in front of their silence, my footsteps echoed off the stage as they continued to sit in silence.

When I hit the last step coming off the landing to go and find my seat, the room exploded in applause and cheers as the teens considered what I'd just shared with them and what God did for me. Their excitement for God went to another level and they had an understanding of the lie. Several came up to me following the event and hugged me so tight I could barely breathe because they'd been considering suicide at one point in time or another. Some kids had lost friends from violence in their home city and were familiar with gun violence and appreciated me sharing with them that even in ugly violence, a person could still turn to God. It meant a lot to them for me sharing my testimony, but it also brought a sense of healing to my life. It took something meant to destroy my life; yet, I helped others and brought glory to God. Many of them became pen pals, and we stayed in touch over the years.

I went to a few more camps and repeated what I did the first time I got up and shared and each time the results were always the same. The other teenagers and some adults were so moved by how God intervened and restored my life. I told them how the bullet broke apart inside of me and went into different directions but missed all of my vital organs. I told them about the voice, hearing the sound of children laughing; waking up finding my face battered and bruised from being dragged across the ground, and how help found me. The more I shared; the seed to a dream was being sown into my life. The dream was to share my testimony, give glory to God and warn people about the beast. I knew the beast was still active because it took two people I knew from my school. My final camp before graduation came; I was pulled aside by some adults and advised I couldn't share with the crowd anymore. The subject matter was too disturbing and controversial. The story happened to me. It was a page torn from my life, and that page was deemed disturbing and controversial. My life was a controversy.

I was growing weary of the way the village was treating me. I had done nothing to them. I made a mistake when I listened to the lie and felt pretty certain I valued my life more than they did. I understood things about life they didn't. I knew I took for granted my health until I got sick. As soon as I was sick with the flu I missed my healthy life and as soon as I felt better, I always had a few days of rejoicing I was no longer bed ridden. What happened to me was on another dimension of thankfulness. The constant hammering on me for what I did was causing me more damage than the reason why I ever shot myself, and I was starting to grow bitter. These adult advisors didn't see what my life was like before my suicide. They weren't with me in the woods before the shot, but God was there. They didn't carry my shattered body out of the woods, but God did. They asked me to sit down as another door was slammed shut on me because of my suicide.

I had contracted social leprosy. At this point so close to graduation, I could see what my options were going to be: Live isolated from the village in the caves or live in the village hiding myself from the villagers. In my final semester of school, my classmates were busy with final preparations to head off to college, and I entered a holding pattern. I wasn't too rattled by the military not accepting me. I had a few years on my hands before I was old enough to realize my dream of being a police man, and I remained hopeful.

YES; I HAVE A HISTORY OF A

SUICIDE ATTEMPT

I graduated high school in the summer of 1988 and had no immediate prospects on the horizon. My friends had gone off to college and I got a car with some car payments. To make the payments, I needed a job. I got a job in a hazy smoke filled lunch room with people twice my age. They were hard working people with mortgage payments and kids in school. Other than my coworkers and family at home, there was no one else in my life. I went to a few churches but I found the same as my work:

older busy people or kids still in school. I worked and went home and sat by myself. Unfortunately, coworkers found out about my shooting. Typically some would see me rubbing my chest because it was throbbing. Some would make crude comments and I'd blurt out that I'd been shot. Typically the next question they asked: *"how?"* I thought because they were older than me they would be more mature and surely they'd be decent, so I told them the truth. I was naïve. Nothing changed. People started looking for the nearest exit, and if they stayed, they'd scoff out of discomfort or shock.

The weeks turned into months and in no time my first year post high school flew past. I still dreaded the month of January, and the center of my chest remained invisible to me. I was lonely in my role as the village monster, and the isolation of the caves wore on me. Occasionally, I wandered into the village and during one such expedition I ran into a pretty girl at a video store when I rented a movie for the weekend. She'd graduated a year of ahead of me, and we hit it off. She invited me to a bible study for young adults and I gladly accepted the offer. Soon the video girl and I were seeing each other on a regular basis and soon spoke of a future together. It was time for me to come out of the caves and live with the villagers.

Six months into my relationship with her, it came time for me to pursue my childhood dream of being a police officer. I turned twenty and six months. It had been over four years since the shooting. I was drug free and alcohol free. I had never been in trouble with the law and my driving record was clean. I had only a couple of jobs since high school and made my car payment on time each month. I was as stable as the next person. I went down to the county human resources office and picked up my application. I filled it out, submitted it, and waited for a testing date. It never entered my mind I may not get hired and I had no other plans should the door not open for me. The hiring process would take three to six months and applicants were weeded out along each step of the way. I got my letter in the mail for the first available testing date. I went and got books on how to take a police aptitude test and started working out so I could pass the physical agility test.

I showed up on the test day and had no trouble passing it. I went for a polygraph exam and back ground check and had no trouble passing any of those. All I had to take was the psychiatric interview, take a physical and wait until I was called up for a final interview. The only obstacle I had to clear was the psychiatric battery, but it'd been five years since my shooting. There was a question on a questionnaire *"Have you ever in the past been treated and or hospitalized for depression?"* Then a few questions later the questionnaire asked *"Have you ever in the past been hospitalized for an attempted suicide?"* I answered the questions truthfully and sat down with the psychologist for an interview. He asked me about my attempted suicide and wanted to know if I still felt suicidal at this point? He wanted to know if there'd been any other thoughts or attempts. I told him I wanted to live and was planning on getting married soon. I knew I had a future and no desire to end my life. I felt like none of the villagers believed me. I wanted to scream at the top of my lungs ***"if I wanted to die that day, I never would've crawled towards help!"*** *I'd already pulled the trigger before and experienced that personal hell. Why would I go through the misery of dialing out another dose of violence in an effort to end my life when I found out, at the end of trail, suicide ultimately lied to me?* The village's logic kept heaping frustration on me. Yes, I understood failed attempts raised future attempts by a steep margin, but my legacy wasn't one of death but one of life! I'd discovered something that day most of the villagers were unaware of: their life was a precious gift. My life was a precious gift made more valuable by the second chance I'd been given, and I wasn't about to squander it by further suicidal efforts. All I wanted to do was get past this suicide and pursue my childhood dream of serving my community as a police officer. I wanted to get married and provide for my wife and start a family with her. The villagers were unwilling to see past my suicide and trust what I was saying to them. Once you cross that line and enter the world of mental illness, you've been marked by the village and are considered *"unclean"*.

The letter came in the mail during the summer like the letter I got from my mother. Her letter had pretty handwriting, but this letter was typed. Her letter smelled like perfume, but this letter was written on official stationary. I tore open the envelope and two words jumped out at me: **We regret.** There was no need to keep reading as I let the letter drop from my hand to the floor. No letter that ever starts with these two words "We regret" ends well for whom the letter is addressed. Another door slammed shut in my face.

I started to feel a strong tremor in the reactor cooling pond as cooling water started to drain off. This was it. This was my childhood dream and because I shot myself five years before, I was too much of a liability. The village felt because I broke in the past, I' break in the future, and I wasn't trustworthy to serve and protect them. My life was a liability to some, controversial and disturbing to others. I wanted to scream and throw things across the house **"My God, what did I do to my life?"** My life had been stolen from me because of suicide. It left me trapped in a scarred body hurting on more days than not. *My life had been laughed, despised, ridiculed and heckled at.* I faced violent and intrusive flashbacks. I was denied a chance to serve my country in the military and to serve my community as a police officer. I was humiliated when I was told I couldn't share publicly what God delivered my life from while other teens were in the process of speaking about what God's miracles had done for them. They asked me to sit down. I had to sit in silence when the master of ceremonies said to the audience as the flow of teens going to the microphone slowed to a trickle *"if anybody else* *feels led to share tonight what God did for your life, now's your chance."* My life was an offense to so many people because I survived a self -inflicted gun- shot wound the day when I wasn't supposed to live to see the next day.

All of the police explorers I'd been friends with were being hired with local police agencies. I was about to be married soon, and I had no way to provide for a new family. I had no idea what else I'd be interested in doing or what my talents were for other possible vocations. It never occurred to me to break off the engagement. I chalked up the rejection as a fluke and began to fire off applications and send resumes to dozens of police agencies. If there was a test I was there for it. I purchased every practice book I could find how to raise my grades on the written test. I worked out to improve my speed and stamina for the agility test but the letters kept flooding back in: "**We regret to inform you**." Sometimes the agency would list automatic disqualifiers on the application packet: "Previous felony convictions, some misdemeanors and any previous hospitalizations for a suicide attempts."

The optimism I felt when I woke up in the hospital in 1986 was long gone. I'd gotten married and under pressure to find a real job, I gave up this notion of ever being a police man. My wife, in- laws and family were yelling at me to give up on my dream. It was recommended I consider health care. It wasn't my first choice, but the income would provide for my new family. I signed up for a two year program, and after I graduated, it confirmed a growing concern I'd been trying to ignore for the last twenty- four months. This was a mistake. Every day I went to work, I was reminded my childhood ambition was denied. I felt like a total failure. I'd found healthcare to be an exacting career, and it was not just a job but a calling. The people closest to my life were trying to force feed me on this thought process this career was good and right for my life based on the merits of its income potential.

I felt uncomfortable in the healthcare environment. The smells, sounds and suffering all kept me on edge. With so many doors slamming shut in my face I had retreated to the caves to protect myself but this had come at a cost. Patients, coworkers complained to my supervisors about my distant and brooding personality. I struggled to multi task the incredible amounts of paperwork. I was falling into a deeper state of depression.

The depression heated up the toxic memory rods at my core, and they started to boil off the cooling water. With some of the rods breaking the surface, I started to have intrusive flashbacks. The flashbacks would further add to my depression. I avoided work at all cost because I dreaded going to work every day. It was not uncommon to have four or five jobs a year. Unable to keep steady work, my marriage and finances started to suffer. My wife and her family spoke openly of their concerns about my inability to provide for her. Many harsh conversations ended with this question: *"What is your problem, and when are you going to grow up and accept some responsibility?"*

It had been almost ten years since I shot myself, and I regained most of my sense of touch over the left side of my body except bullet scar. I also accepted the outward scars as part of me. For the most part I felt numb, and if I weren't numb, I was depressed under a cloud. I hadn't seen a counselor since high school and rarely went to church let alone prayed or spent time with God. My life had been stolen from me. I shot myself as a consequence of living my life in a painful, depressed state. I entertained suicidal thoughts for the first time as a result of a panic attack one afternoon at the thought of having to face my father. I felt invisible to the world from the time I went into the first grade because my mother walked away and a stepmother whom admitted to me, she turned away. Ultimately in spite of it all, the responsibility for loading the rifle and pulling the trigger rested with me because I was paying the price and no one else. A lot of wrongs had been done to me as a child, but when I pulled the trigger it no longer mattered because those reasons died that day.

My depressed child hood was a record for the history books, but here in the present day, my *"botched suicide"* was as much of my everyday reality as the scar across my back. I had emotional bills to pay, and there weren't enough resources in my bank to pay for them. I started to feel a deep emotional burn in the center of my life. I was becoming afraid of a flash of light containing a chunk of metal. The more depressed I became the more real the memory of the light cloaking the metal became to me and I needed to find a way to cool the reactor's core before the light's metal ripped into me once more. The only thing my brain cared about was keeping the memory of the light and its metal away from me. I started making irrational life choices in an effort to find equilibrium in my life. The stress and depression were making my post-traumatic stress symptoms severe. I had to find a way to reduce the stress or the PTSD symptoms would get more severe.

I avoided work as much as possible and only worked on a part time basis or on an as- needed agreement. If I worked more than a few days a week then that many times was too much. This reduced the flow of income into my home and caused problems at home. I enrolled in a community college in a way to further my healthcare career. It was a career I never wanted and whenever I passed a police officer working, I still admired them as much as I did when I drew a picture and sent my picture to our local police department. I hated feeling physically weak and broken so I joined a local gym.

For the first time I found something I was good at. My body started to change before my eyes and I no longer felt physically broken or weak. I studied nutrition and ways to pack muscle onto my frame. I felt positive about myself and noticed the light hiding the metal wasn't as bright anymore as chilled water flooded the hazardous memories. My core started to cool down. My brain found an outlet to protect myself, and this was the only thing I cared about at the expense of everything else. One unintended consequence for spending so much time in the gym and transforming my body was, I started to receive attention. Since I had been invisible all of my life this attention became my heroin addiction. Girls started to approach me at school, work, gym, restaurants and shopping malls. I found an escape from my depression. Instead of turning to suicide to relieve me of my emotional pain I looked for this new addiction to escape my depressed failed life. My suicidal ideations became an addiction, and coming with a high cost, this addiction was no different. It came at a price, and it also lied to me.

I felt guilty for flirting with the girls I came across or when I took a phone number. I knew I was rebelling against the truth, and I'd turned my life away from God. I had met a few compassionate people in my life that knew my story and they would often say *"God surely has a plan for your life."* I looked at my broken, shattered, ugly past and wanted to scream at them and God, **"I don't see it! I mean surely I missed an exit somewhere!"** If I turned and faced God and repented of this addiction, that would mean I had to face the stress. The stress boiled the water away, and with the water gone, the bullet was no longer suspended in time hidden within the muzzle flash. It would continue on towards its intended target, and that was something my brain would never permit. I gave up on church because I knew the addiction was wrong, and I couldn't bear to be around my brother and sisters in Christ. I knew they would tell me to surrender all to God, but they didn't know about my past. They didn't know there was a bullet cloaked inside of a white- hot light, and it always came for me if I got too depressed in life.

Ten years after my shooting I tried one more time to become a police officer. I had to accomplish this. If I could kick the door open to this career, that meant suicide was in the past and I'd lived past it. My body survived the shooting but my life had not. I started to move through the hiring process and was doing very well. I had no criminal record and no suicidal relapses. I'd completed two years of health care training and had been married for six years so, in my opinion, I was very stable and had overcome a couple of serious challenges in my life. It was a make it or break moment for me. I'd been trying for five years and applied twenty- five times to get a job in law enforcement. I did worse on that day then I did the first time I ever invested eight hours of my life taking the test.

He said there were signs of extreme amount of stress in my life and I was unfit. *It was over.* I'd wanted to be a police officer for no less than twenty years. Ten years prior, someone pulled me aside and offered helpful advice when they recommended I try looking for another career because of the *botched* suicide. I was given a mark, deemed unfit and a liability to my village. It was a hard day when I had to cut the dream loose.

It was during this time I got a phone call from my father. When I moved out of the house, I rarely had contact with him unless he wanted me to come help him with something. It didn't matter if I had something planned with my wife or not. He demanded I come out to the house and help him and remind me of my role. He was my father and I remained his head of cattle. If he wanted something, he demanded I hand it over to him. If he wanted something done, then he insisted I drop what I was doing to come take care of whatever he wanted done. If I resisted because I had prior plans, he would blow up and hammer me over the phone.

During this particular phone call he sounded different. He insisted I come see him right away, and I was to be alone. I ignored his request and I brought my wife along. When I arrived, he was sitting in the kitchen and asked my wife and stepmother to leave the two of us alone for a few hours. When they left, he went into his study and came back with a brief case. He opened the brief case and inside there were several bottles of prescription medications and a semi-automatic handgun. I glanced at the prescription medications and knew from experience, they were psychotropic prescriptions. He started to ramble on about regrets in his life. I was ok with him being open about regrets; what worried me was the demonstration of the handgun between the two of us. He could've been open and honest with me over a glass of lemonade on the front porch; not here with a gun and prescription medication. For the third time in my life, this man made me feel unsafe. It started when he threatened me about learning to ride a bike over rocks. Then he shut the truck the truck off at night in the middle of a well-traveled section of highway. Now, I sat with him and his handgun. The lights were out in his eyes and some of the conversation was lucid and coherent. Other times he would lose his train of thought and pick up another idea. After a half hour, the lights went back on and he closed the brief case to put it away.

As a father, I can't begin to attempt to reconcile what the night of my shooting must've done to my family. I would never wish the destructive force on an enemy, let alone on the people who provided for me. We are all human and subject to the same sinful nature and make mistakes. Some repent of their mistakes while others choose not to. Good bad or indifferent, they were my family and my heart continues to mourn for a broken family.

I was full- time college student eleven years after my shooting. I lived at the gym or in the student lounge. I avoided my wife and home at all cost. A smile or flirtatious comment made the world a better place. The more attention I got the more I dove into body building. Unfortunately like any addiction, this addiction also required a higher dose to keep the desired effect in place. It was the beginning of a new semester and only the second time in a new math class. I had to get up and go to the professor's desk, and as I walked down the aisle, I made eye contact with a very attractive person my age. She smiled at me as I walked past her and my heart stopped beating. After class, she followed me down the hall towards the student lounge and started to strike up a conversation with me. For the better part of the day, we sat and talked in the lounge. She told me she was divorced and lived across town. She'd moved to the US after meeting her husband while he was serving in the military in Europe. I was taken aback by her beauty and forwardness with me. She could have had any available man in the county and probably some that should have been off limits. The attention I'd been getting over the years was one form of a narcotic, but the attention my new friend was showing me took this addiction to another level. I wasn't a shot up reanimated village monster in her eyes; in fact; she wasn't interested in my past as she invited me to her house. My brain leaped at the chance because the core was flooding with chilled water, and the reactor was going into the green. The bullet and the flash of light were gone. I felt like I did when I went to the church camp the summer before I shot myself. I wanted to put as much distance from my reality and run away with this beautiful and available girl. I resisted her advances for a couple of weeks but each time I spoke with her I gave up more ground when I should have turned and ran for my life when she first introduced herself to me. I broke my marriage vow five years after I promised to forsake all others. I ended the relationship with the girl, but the damage had been done.

I was crushed and ashamed of myself. The affair reminded me of my suicide. It promised so much, and it never mentioned the consequences. I hid myself from my wife for a long time for what I'd done. I wasn't going anywhere with my life. I told her I wanted to pursue another educational program, and her frustration mounted. She wanted children, stability and a husband who cared for her.

Almost a full year after I had an affair one day, I was on my way to the gym and my part-time job as a mall security guard. I liked the job because it was low stress, and it gave me the chance to hit all of the stores in the mall to flirt with countless female employees of those stores. I didn't think it was a big deal because I knew I wasn't going to actually cheat on my wife again, but I still needed my drug of choice to keep the muzzle flash away. As I drove along, there was a stern loving confrontation, and it was so powerful I had to pull the car over. It had been a long time since I heard this voice. I was a rebellious son and had grieved the only source of true love I'd ever known. My heart was so broken I was willfully grieving the loving God who saved my life. I looked at my face in the rearview mirror and reflected. Though I was hurting in my life, I did not have the right to cause collateral damage to other people's lives. I repented in my heart and to God. I made a life change and felt my relationship with God re-established. He was true to His word so I confessed my sin and like the wayward son, He came to me and greeted me. I didn't go to the gym. When I went to work that night, I didn't make any of my usual stops. My life had peace and joy in it for the first time in a long time. However, what I didn't know was the beast was about to challenge my commitments as it found a way to breach the reactors core and drain the life protecting water away from me.

.

MELTDOWN

While I'd been emotionally absent for a couple of years, I'd discovered a new love for my wife when I made this turn around. She had made some changes as well. The summer after my affair, she had made a career change of her own. She had been in healthcare with me as well. She'd encouraged me to take on the health care career but after a few years she made the career change into law enforcement. I felt my first strong tremor in the reactor because I'd quit my job at the mall and chose to not to go back to college in the fall so I could focus on our marriage. When I was going to work at a career I struggled with the very first day I graduated from school, she was going to a police academy. She'd succeeded at what I failed at so many times, and she succeeded on her first try. I was determined to not let this get the best of me, and the nasty irony the beast was flaunting in my face. She'd worked hard to get hired and based on my experience with God and His love for me, I knew love gave and never took. So I focused on how proud I was for her and encouraged her in her career.

In the past, she wanted to go to church, but I avoided church. After I had repented to God I wanted to be back in worship with her and fellow brother and sisters. I noticed something odd, she avoided going. She never wanted to go to church and this wasn't like her. I also noticed she wasn't around the house anymore and avoided looking me in the eyes. There were moments of erratic behavior on her part I shrugged off. She went for a bag of potato chips before we went to a picnic, and she was gone for two hours. When she came back home I asked her if she was ok and why it took so long? Her response was the line was too long, and I shrugged it off and said ok.

I was working full- time and home when I wasn't working. I rarely went to the gym and sought to spend time with her. She started to find other things to argue with me over. I'd had my heart in the right place for a few months. I knew I needed to confess my affair to her the summer before and was trying to figure out how to tell her, but I noticed she wasn't there anymore or like she would even care. One rainy night, she started to argue with me over yet another small issue that was something that never bothered her before. Someone suggested a separation and, in short order, I found myself on the street with my suitcase in disbelief. I couldn't understand what just hit me. I had grown into the man she'd wanted from the day we started to consider a future together. I was responsible, and I'd come to terms with my past. I loved her and was committed to our future, but she was gone. A few weeks after our separation I finally understood what was happening. She was involved with another person. This thought smashed into the reactor like an enemy cruise missile seeking to take out a hard target. It had been going on for a few months, and I found a letter. The reactor was in full meltdown.

I could feel the rifle in my hands again though my hands were empty. This was what my mind had been trying to protect me from for the last ten years, seeing and living it again. I could feel the bolt action in my hands.

Then I saw my younger hands remove the safety. I could see my grey slacks with the rifle lying across my lap. I watched helplessly as I picked up the rifle from my lap and put the barrel next to my heart. I collapsed into a fetal position and started to sob, begging myself to stop. I knew what was going to happen next, and there was no escaping it. I wasn't lying in our bedroom on our bed with a love letter from my wife to her friend; I was standing in the woods next to a naïve teenager. The beast was on the other side of the veil ready to devour this teenager wearing the light blue coat. The boy couldn't see what I saw because he didn't realize he had been lied to. The beast was glaring at the teenager because he hated him. He wanted to kill him. It wanted to destroy his life, and the lives of everyone the teenager knew from the grief his suicide would surely cause. I ran up to the side of the teenager and howled at him to not pull the trigger. The beast no longer glared at the boy, but turned its yellow hatred filled eyes and smiled at me. It whispered *"I killed you once before; watch as I do it again."*

The boy pulled the trigger and once more I felt my chest implode as I whaled in grief from the pain. The beast stood over my writhing body as I could smell my blood as fresh as I did in 1986. The reactor exploded, and the beast spit in my face. I started to panic and got in my car and drove all night long.

I called my wife and told her what was going on. She knew I knew of her affair, but she was concerned for my mental health asked I check myself into a mental health unit. I drove to the same hospital I almost died at and told them I was suicidal. I wasn't, but what I saw the night before seemed so real and frightening I felt I was. I hadn't smelled that much blood since the shooting and knew the reactor was on fire. I slept for a week, sat in group, and made chocolate chip cookies. At the end of the week they gave me my shoelaces back, and I went on my way. I met up with my wife and confessed my affair with her. We tried for a year to reconcile things. We went to counseling and moved to a new home to shake off bad memories. We would separate for a couple of months and try again, but too many stress fractures were there. She encouraged me to finish my degree.

Eleven years after my shooting I had a full-time job and was attending college full-time. My marriage had been destroyed, and my faith in God waivered again. I was angry with myself for doing the right thing the summer before. If I'd been self-absorbed with my girlfriend's life, I don't think my wife's affair would've had the impact it had on me. The girlfriend would've been a distraction, and the blow of her affair would've been a glancing shot as opposed to me catching it in the center of my being. When my head hit the pillow at night and I when I was alone with my thoughts, I did feel a sense of strength though. Though I was angry at myself for opening myself up to pain because I'd cut myself off from my emotional pain medication just prior to receiving devastating news, I had learned a valuable lesson. I had grown as a human being though my life was a wreck. I learned no matter how badly I hurt I didn't have the right to take from another person's life. Just because I was miserable, I didn't have the right to make other people's lives equally miserable. I didn't have the right to cheat on my wife because I had unmet needs in my life. This was the second vow I made to myself: *I'd never die from suicide and I'd never mistreat another person in my life because of my personal giants.* This life lesson didn't do a lot of good at this point because it was like showing up a day late and dollar short.. It seemed like a valuable lesson so I tucked it away inside of my heart. To the average observer during that time, it seemed my life was a mess. It was eleven years after my battle with the beast and I was still upright and walking. It had left some terrible wounds in my life, but it never got me.

A month after my wife moved out for the last time, the lease to our home expired and there was no point in living there by myself. If I could hold on until the end of the year, I'd graduate and see a large income boost. I could get a nice apartment on my own and try to start my life over again. My wife agreed to cover some of my expenses so I could focus on school. My challenge was to find a place to live until I graduated school. The two semesters before graduation consisted of clinical work at local hospitals and healthcare centers. It was a forty hour work week with no pay. Then I worked thirty two hours over the weekend.

I moved in with distant family for a month then move with a friend of friend. I slept in basements and couches. Some weekends, I slept at work. They would find a place for me to sleep between my two sixteen hour shifts. I made it through one semester bouncing around from house to house. The second semester started, and it was twelve years after my shooting. I was exhausted and constantly faced intrusive violent memories because there was no coolant protecting my toxic post-traumatic memories.   When I was at school I had trouble concentrating.   When I was at work, I had trouble concentrating. I missed my soon-to-be ex-wife and gotten the impression she'd moved on to someone who was stable, unlike me. My academic career was in a nose dive. My health was suffering too I contracted pneumonia that winter and lost a considerable amount of weight. I was tired from sleeping in a different house every few nights. I was barely hanging on, and my instructors were trying to encourage me to hang on because graduation was only a few months away.

One night, I had run out of places to stay. I found myself sleeping in my car behind a grocery store and woke up to a garbage truck picking up the dumpster near me. It was time to make a phone call I'd been dreading. I called home and asked if I could move in until I graduated. My father said I could move in but had to be gone by the time I graduated. For the first time since, I graduated I moved home with nothing to my name but a few trash bags full of clothes.

One day six weeks before graduation, I was on my way to class when an impulse hit me. I pulled my car into the median strip and sat for a few minutes. I didn't realize how exhausted I had become. I needed rest more than anything in life. I couldn't keep it up any longer. My life was more valuable than a college degree. I wasn't going to die over a college degree. I knew my past struggle, and I knew that battle had fractured me. The police agencies were right in not hiring me. The village was right about my life. They told me I would break at some point in the future and here I was sitting in the middle of the highway watching cars fly past. I didn't have health insurance to go see a mental health provider. I was alone in life. My wife was gone, and my father wanted me out of his house. If I didn't start yanking some irons out of the fire, then my past was going to catch up to me. I knew I had it in me, and it scared me. I didn't have a buddy system to keep me alive. I honored my personal vow and waited for a safe place to pull out and drove away from college. I just quit college with less than two months to go, but I was alive. The village erupted when they heard the monster quit his classes. They screamed and yelled at me for being a losing quitter. It bothered me to a degree that I had to make an irrational and abrupt change so close to the finish line, but I knew I couldn't keep the pace up any longer and my life mattered. Shortly after I dropped out of college, I came home one day to find my belongings out in the street. My father cleaned out my clothes, placed them in trash bags and tossed them outside to punish me for quitting college. I picked up my bags and threw them in my car. I was homeless, but I was alive.

A SAFE HARBOR

Prior to being thrown out of the house, I'd applied to sell gym memberships. I knew my history, and the stress had eroded that buffer over the years. The villagers had lit torches and were rallying against my life because they didn't understand the monster. They saw an irrational man quit college and a good paying career all in the same month. Several people from the village told me to just get over my shooting and move on. They'd never been through my personal battle but felt the best advice for me was to think positive thoughts and not dwell on the past.

They never understood I couldn't escape my own body's past.

I wanted to wheel a chalk board into the center of the village and ask if I could have everyone's attention for a few minutes. Once the village slowed down to see what the monster was up to, I'd pick up a piece of chalk and draw a glove on the board. I'd then tell them this story: *Once upon a time a worker lost something of tremendous value in a fire. He had to retrieve the thing that was lost and knew he had to reach into the fire to save his valuable. He felt his hand would have some protection because like all the workers in the factory, he wore a pair of gloves. Without further hesitation, the worker plunged his hand into the fire, but he wasn't able to reach the valuable at first and had to struggle under an immense searing pain longer than first anticipated. The worker never imagined the pain would be this severe because he'd never been under such stress before so there wasn't anything he could compare this moment to. After a few moments of an intense struggle, the worker grasped the valuable and his hand was removed from the fire. The worker's hand was in a tremendous amount of pain and the glove was smoldering and damaged as a result of the trauma. The*

worker removed his hand from the glove and without the energy from the hand the glove went limp and lifeless. The glove cools down and once it's cool enough the hand goes back into the glove. The glove comes back to life, and the worker mends the glove back to its pre fire condition. This is the only pair issued, and he is unable to swap it out for a new pair. The other workers see the repaired glove and insist the worker keep up with them. No one in the company can see how the workers' hand remains in pain following its time in the fire. They question why he struggles with basic tasks and why he favors the one hand. They grow irritated with him when he takes longer to complete task and start to insult him. They tell him he should be over the trauma of the fire because the glove is fine. The company threatens to terminate him because he is slow and incompetent. The worker needs his job and tries as hard as he can to keep up but his hand continues to feel the heat of the fire though his hand has not been in the fire for some time. The company is forced to let him go.
I'd scribble out under my drawing of the glove these words
"Post -Traumatic Stress Disorder"

Without knowing it, my subconscious mind knew my illness better than anyone including me. The stress of the last few years had eroded my buffer to my past locked inside of me. My subconscious mind kept my core under constant supervision. It knew in June 1985 as a result of environmental stress, considered suicide for the first time. *I'd been in a fire for a very long time and though my body appeared fine my hand was in a tremendous amount of pain.* The years of living in the destructive environment had taken its toll on me, and the suicide was my way of removing my spirit out from my body. *When I got into the fire, I didn't realize it was going to be as bad as it was because I had nothing in my past to prepare me for the moment.* When I pulled the trigger, nothing on this earth could've prepared me for what I was about to see and experience. *My body was pulled from the fire of trauma and just like the hand leaving the glove my sprit left my body.* I either touched the veil separating life and death or I penetrated the other side for a moment, but the astronauts continued on. *The glove was cooled and mended so the hand could continue and take on shape and life again.* The efforts of the medical team saved my life that night, and the scars bear this fact. *The workers saw the glove had been repaired and assumed he should keep up with them.* At every turn from the moment I graduated high school I struggled to provide a stable life for myself and my ex-wife. I had been working out, and by every appearance, I was strong and healthy. *The workers hand continued to feel the fire of the trauma long after the flames were gone.* It had been over ten years, but I could still feel the effects of the trauma as though it was as recent as last week's headlines. *The company begins to threaten the worker with termination because he is unable to keep up with the other workers.* I was unable to keep up with the demands of life in a modern society because none of the reasons why I shot myself were ever addressed. None of the symptoms that come with post - traumatic stress were ever addressed. I had all of normal stress of life in a modern society in addition to the other baggage I was trying to figure out how to carry. *Unable to keep up with his peers and never taking into consideration the workers hand has been scarred as a result of the trauma, the company cuts ties.* Unable to keep all of the balls in the air I had to juggle, my life personal life collapsed.

This time it was not the summer of 1985. It was the summer of 1998. The fire was burning my hand like it was doing in the summer of 1985, and my subconscious mind had been keeping vigil since 1986 for such a time as this. It knew my disease process, and it knew I turned to suicidal thoughts like an alcoholic turns to alcohol to medicate life's woes. Unlike an alcoholic that may suffer a relapse, if I should suffer a relapse, it could cost me my life. With my gloved hand in the fire, my subconscious mind made my will to live pull out a wild card I'd never saw coming. Instead of pulling my hand out of the fire, the other hand found a bucket of water and poured the entire bucket of water all over the fire and doused the fire.

In order to cut the stress from my life and knowing my history, I doused the flames of stress with a bucket of water. I quit college, my marriage, my career and didn't really care anymore the village was angry with me. I didn't have access to mental health care or a healthy support system, and I knew I was in danger again like I was in 1985. I knew what was on the other side of the fence, and I wasn't going back over the wall. By drastically reducing my stress and willing to face the consequences, I fought for my life ultimately. My immediate social circle didn't understand, and at the time, neither did I. All I knew I was still alive and that was all I cared about.

I'd gotten the job selling gym memberships but not in my local community. The manager of the gym forwarded my application to a sister gym about forty miles north in another state. I went up and interviewed, and I was offered a job. At first, I was disappointed, but my attitude shifted when I considered it was an opportunity to start fresh in a community not loaded with memory triggers. No one knew my past, and I felt at peace. Though I didn't have a place to live, deep down I knew I was going to be ok. My core was no longer stressed and everything remained at a safe level. I needed to figure out how I was going to find a place to sleep and shower until I saved enough money to get my own apartment. I'd taken a cut in pay when I left the health care career, but I was better off with a lower stressed job that paid less than the rigors of a higher paying job and have my core breached and hit critical mass and my life threatened again.

I stumbled upon a way to find shelter during the few months I had to live out of my car. I'd work all day and go to the clubs at night. Some nights, I went home with someone and found a place to sleep. It was better than trying to sleep in a car and I couldn't afford to spend money on a motel room. In the morning, I'd go back to work, exercise, shower, and start my shift. I was forced to eat out, but when I did eat out I didn't eat much. My lonely life and depression had taken away my appetite. If I couldn't find anyone to go home with, I'd sleep in my car. The worst time of the week was Sunday through Tuesday. The clubs were closed Sunday through Tuesday, and that meant I was forced to sleep in my car three nights in a row. If I had the weekend off from the gym, then I was bound to the car for most of the weekend. With no home to go sit and prop my feet up, there was no place to just sit and be still. The only toilet to be found was at a truck stop, and my closet was the trunk of the car packed with plastic trash bags holding my few possessions. I passed my free time by driving the interstates between my new "home" state and my former state. Many nights, I would drive around my former state and places I used to call home thankful I was no longer going to call the state home. A place full of terrible memory triggers. When I got tired of driving, I would find a place to sleep behind a store and sleep a few hours. Then get up and do it all over again until the sun came up. If the sun came up and I was off from the gym, I found some parking lots provided a safe place to get a few hours of solid sleep. No one paid any attention to me as they walked passed me. I remember thinking I could be dead, and no one would know.

One night, I was sitting in my car just before midnight in a desolate parking lot trying to keep a low profile and a vigilant eye out for the police. I knew I was suspicious looking even though I knew I was harmless. I was some guy who didn't have a place to sleep for the night. I had a cup of coffee for company and was listening to an old friend. It was the radio station I'd tuned into twelve years before when I was recovering from my gunshot wound. I was enjoying the radio station's company when I heard a tap on the window.

Startled, I looked up over my shoulder through the driver's side window, and there, standing next to me, was the *beast.* Its yellow eyes burned through me, and it smiled the same grin I saw the night I found my ex-wife's letter to her friend and in my flashback, I saw it waiting for me on the other side of the veil. I'd seen the beast many times as it paid a visit to other lives. When I opened the news-paper and I read of a suicide in our community, I knew I'd probably see it leaving town or perhaps lurking in the shadows to claim another. No one saw this lying creature until it was too late, and I had many nightmares about it over the years. One of the common nightmares, I found myself walking down a path when I came to a high wall. It was impossible to see over the other side. There were signs posted, *"**Warning, No Trespassing**"* I wanted off this path since the other side seemed so inviting. So I climbed over the fence and ignored the clearly posted warnings. I reached the other side of the fence and wasn't over there but only a moment when the beast stepped out from behind a tree and started to sprint towards me with its mouth wide open seeking to devour me. I turned and tried to climb back over the wall but it was easier to cross over to this side then get back over to the safety of the other side. I looked over my shoulder and since the beast was good at transforming its shape, it had turned into the largest dog I'd ever seen as it started to lunge for me. The dog got its jaws into my chest and started to crush me with its teeth when I called out for help. A hand reached down and grabbed my arm and pulled me to safety and back over the wall. I landed firmly on the other side bleeding and bruised, but I would live. To my horror, I saw people walking this same path I did. I saw them ignore the same warning signs and climb over the wall and drop out of sight. It was always quiet but I knew what was on the other side of the wall. Very few came back over to this side. If they could see through my eyes what I saw when I went over, they would think twice about it and go a different way. It reminded me of my past and told me no one would know I was gone. It told me no one cared enough to offer me a place to stay until I got back on my feet. It also started to whisper doubts and questions about my future. Suppose my life wasn't going to get better? Suppose I couldn't pull myself back up off the ground again? Perhaps, I made a terrible mistake by coming out of the woods that day. It reminded me the village always told me would perhaps break. They were right as it picked its teeth and winked at me. It climbed up on the hood of my car and looked into the windshield at me and gazed into my face and laughed. It said to me, *"The true shame of it all. You went through all of that trouble of shooting yourself; you're going to have to do it all over again."*

I looked down at my cup of coffee and back up through the windshield. There was no beast sitting on the hood of my car. The beast existed in my thoughts, memories and in its world on the other side of the veil. That violent world suicide never reveals to its victims. I was alone in life. I had no guarantee my life was going to get better. I looked at my eyes in the rearview mirror and could hear the siren song. There was nowhere for a homeless person to go in the middle of a Sunday Night to get help. It was me, alone in the world, with my past in the middle of the night in an isolated parking lot. I had an advantage over the beast and at this vulnerable point in my life; I needed to take the advantage. I knew what was on the other side. I was not naïve anymore and heeded the warnings clearly posted to stay away. I used the intrusive and violent flashback to keep me alive that night. I didn't want to go back over the wall ever again. I made a promise to myself many years ago, and it was being put to the test. Just like a sober alcoholic may hear his past call out to him, sobriety has a sweeter sound. The beast could kick the side of the car all it wanted. My life may be in the gutter but I was still alive and had the pleasure of a nice cup of coffee and that was something worth living for. I smiled at myself in my cramped car because I knew in my heart, I wasn't ever going back over that wall. The beast may show back in my memories and kick **its** own cage, but it never got my life.

After two months of this cycle, God provided a home for me. I knew what it was to be homeless and have my vow tested in the middle of a dark night with no support group, and I stood up under it. One day at work, I met two guys who were members there. They had noticed I was new and not from the area, and they approached me one afternoon. After we introduced ourselves, they explained to me they were looking to lease an apartment. They had made plans on getting a two bedroom apartment, but they really wanted a three bedroom unit. The only way they could take on a three bed room unit would be if they got a third roommate. I was floored when they asked me if I would be interested in going in on the lease with them. I wanted to run, jump and shout for joy. My circumstances were changing. The beast had tested my resolve and I stood my ground. Then here, a few weeks later out of the nowhere two guys offered me a room. They explained to me it would be another month before we could move into the apartment, and they asked me my present living situation. I explained to them it was very "fluid" at the moment. One of the two explained to me his situation was not as fluid as mine, but I was welcomed to crash where he did. He was a manager at an older movie theater, and it had an office off an upstairs balcony. He called dibs on the cot but the overstuffed movie chairs did recline back enough to provide for a reasonably comfortable night's rest. He said I could stay there with him until our apartment was ready. I was no longer sleeping in my car and no longer trying to find a different bed or couch to sleep in most other nights. To me, the movie theater was a five star resort after the ordeal I had just lived through. God had provided shelter for me and I was still alive.

I never imagined I'd find shelter in a movie theater for a season, but it was fun for a month. I got to enjoy free movies and eat all of the popcorn I wanted. I got a job as a bouncer in a nightclub not far from the movie theater. It provided a steady source of income for me, and I kept the job for over two years. The job was low-stress, and it permitted me to get something I needed and that was rest. The attention I got working as a nightclub bouncer medicated and continued to calm my nerves. Since I'd left high school, I found myself: depressed, numb, distant or angry. When a girl handed me her phone number or asked to come home with me, it filled a need in my life.

The relationships were always a dead end and the most serious relationship lasted two months.

I felt safe and the reactor was well cooled. I almost never thought about my shooting anymore unless a girl asked me where I got my scars from. I always told them from a hunting accident. I was among fellow travelers in the nightclub. No one was pushing me to finish my degree or take on more continuing educational classes. The village wasn't around telling me to run out and buy a bigger home. I stayed out late with my new bouncer friends and slept in the next day. I didn't work in the gym because the pay wasn't worth it and it was extremely boring. What I earned working in the nightclubs was enough to pay the rent and utilities and left me with a couple of dollars to try and feed myself. To me, I was getting rest and that was what I needed at this point in my life.

I'd been at the same address for two years and had not had a steady relationship since my ex-wife and I separated two years before. At this point in my life, had been thirteen years since my shooting. I had most of the feeling in my body other than the bullet scar. Occasionally, the old scars would throb but had gotten used to it. The month of January didn't bother me anymore and there were few triggers around my new community for me to worry about. I only saw my family on Christmas Day, but for the rest of the year they never called me and, likewise, I never called them. I know they were more active in my sibling's lives than mine, but that was the way it was when I was growing up so nothing had changed.

I was turning thirty soon and started to feel it was time to step back into the village as a citizen and not the monster hiding in the caves I perceived myself to be when my central core had been taxed. I decided the first thing I should do is stop seeing girls in the nightclub and even consider leaving the business and going back into healthcare. There was plenty of water over the rods and no threat of a meltdown. It was a good time to venture back out into the world and give life another chance. It didn't take long for my resolve to get tested. I had promised I was not going to involve myself with girls from the nightclub I worked at.

One Saturday Night I met her. I was taken aback how beautiful she was. I felt like a diamond miner that'd been working in the dark caves for so long and by just one random swing came across the most beautiful diamond out of all of the diamonds. She was a friend of friend and it was her first time out in a night club, and she ended up at the club I worked at. She shook my hand and we stood and talked about pancakes and other breakfast foods most of the night. She was a single mom, and she rarely got out. Her priority was her daughter and her daughter was away for the weekend with her grandparents. She was a committed mom, and I knew in my heart this was a feature I found desirable. She gave me her phone number, but I wanted to honor my commitment that I was going to change course and not pursue the dead end relationships. So I lost her phone number, but in a couple of weeks I ran into her again. She was just as polite and put together, and I couldn't let this chance pass so I asked for her number again. This time I really did lose her number and happened into her a third time, but this time I went to her and asked for her number. It took some convincing on my part, but she gave in and warned me this was the last time. I went and wrote her number down on several different places so I didn't lose it again. I called her and she invited me to her apartment for dinner and that was an amazing offer because other than Thanksgiving it had been two years since I had a home cooked dinner. When I arrived at her apartment, I realized not only did she allow me into her life but the life of her three year old daughter. I fell in love with both of them from the moment I met them. Her daughter greeted and me and chatted with me through the night.

A year after we met, my wife and I were married. Fourteen years after I sought to release my life with a pull of a trigger, I started my life over once more. We were married in the fall of 2000. Three years prior to this day, my life's ship was lost in a terrible storm. I drifted out at sea for a season and finally washed ashore in nothing more than a rubber raft and the clothes on my back. In the summer of 1998 just two and half years prior to this day, I was living out of my car struggling with thoughts of despair. When I was a teenager, suicidal thoughts became my addiction and drug of choice to manage moments like this. While sitting in my car in a dark isolated parking lot in the middle of the night, my old addiction came knocking at my door. It questioned my future and told me there was no hope. It doubted I would be able to find a safe harbor. The cup of coffee in my hand was warm and the flavor was good. I knew the truth. I fought back this lie. I told the despair life is a gift and worth the struggle. I agreed everything my eyes told me: there seemed to be no point going on. I had not quit on my life. If the only joy I could find in my life was in this cup of coffee then I had found a reason to live and hope for another cup of coffee the next day. If I were dead, then I'd been denying myself a good cup of coffee. *Never give up on yourself. Even if the only thing you can think of is a good cup of coffee then it means you're still alive to look forward to another good cup of coffee the next day.*

After three years, God brought my life into safe harbor. My old addiction had come to challenge my resolve. It pushed and pressed, but I fought it back with truth and hope. The truth is suicide is a lie and no matter how dark the night may seem or violent the storm, the sun eventually comes back. My ship went under in the fall of 1997. and it took three years to tie up in this safe harbor beneath the sun high in the sky with the storm a distant memory.

LIFE IN THE VILLAGE

My wife knew of my history. She looked past the suicide and saw a man she wanted to spend the rest of her life with. A year after we were married, I had lived with a personal knowledge of the beast for over fifteen years. I knew about things such as: living as a reanimated monster, the caves, villagers, the toxic rods and the need to keep them under chilled water to avoid a meltdown. My new wife knew of my past but had not been initiated into the world I'd been living with almost half of my life.

She saw my scars, but she didn't know my life before the scars. She didn't really know about cracking the veil, and the only way I could live was to have my body ravaged with a surgeon's scalpel. She wasn't there the first time I saw my bullet whole pulse next to my heart, and she didn't know shrapnel had been left next to my spine. She rarely saw anyone react when I told people about what I'd survived and been delivered from. It was a secret I protected with my life. She didn't know about the village and how afraid I was of the people who lived there. To me, the village had always been the other side of the wall. It was a wall of stigma attached to any mental health issues. When it came to surviving a serious effort to end my life from the end of a gun, I found a wall of shame almost impregnable. The only way I could pass through the gate and into the village was to hide my past. If my true past ever came out, the gate was sealed shut, and I was kept outside. To me the villagers had been anyone who had a negative reaction to my past. They'd were friends, family, teachers, coworkers, friend's parents and acquaintances. I found villagers in schools, youth camps, churches, cookouts, work, and in my own home. The reactions ranged from a silent icy gaze, disbelieving reactions about my own life's experience with suicide and an occasional tip on how to not botch the next suicide. My new wife didn't know about how damaging the toxic memory rods that were under the reactors cooling water.

As long as the rods were under water then her husband's life was safe. When she met me I had been resting for a couple of years and there was time to replenish the coolant. My wife didn't know about post-traumatic stress disorder nor did I at the time. I knew the memories could range from an unpleasant sensation to memories so powerful they ripped me from my current place in time and made me believe I was back in the woods once more. The ones where my reality became confused had the ability to put me in the hospital because my mind actually believed I was on my way to shoot myself once more and there was nothing I could do stop it.

My new family needed to live in the village and not outside of the wall in caves. So I covered my face with a cloak, hid my past, and walked through the gates. I worried about life's stress and its effects on my core, but I loved my new family so I held my breath. Over the years when I tried to live on the other side of the wall in the village, I learned a few ground rules to protect myself. The first was easy enough to remember: never speak of the suicide. In the days prior to my family if my core gave me problems and I couldn't keep the secret anymore, I could run back to the other side of the wall and seek shelter of the cave. With a new family, I had to adhere to this rule.

The next rule makes living by the first rule easier to live with: Act like it never happened. By living as it never happened, I could avoid the memory triggers. When a memory trigger happened, it would set off a flashback. Sometimes talking through a PTSD flashback is the same as a diabetic getting a shot of insulin when their sugars are high. If I couldn't talk of the suicide, then I needed to protect myself against all triggers. I was always in a heightened state of alert protecting against all triggers.

The next rule: I had to respect my limitations. In order to keep the destructive toxic nature of the core at a safe level for my life, I needed to respect my environmental stress. On two occasions in my life the core had been breached, and both times the results were severe. The first time was in the summer of 1985. The years of despair, fear, and depression cumulated with the panic attack. This panic attack cracked the core and it led to my shooting. Child abuse can lead to a form of post-traumatic stress disorder. The second time the core was breached was in fall of 1996 eventually leaving me homeless. This was also caused by the lingering effects of post -traumatic stress disorder. Across the village square they have a motivational banner hung up for all to see and it consist of one word: **"MORE"**

Even on the best of days, life inside the village is stressful. We get sick, kids get sick and the dog gets sick on the carpet. The tax person finds more ways to tax while miles pile on both our cars and our lives. When we finish the day's task, we are greeted by a new day with fresh tasks to complete and the treadmill never stops. The banner proclaims loudly from the village: **"MORE!"** So if you want to be a productive villager and fit in, then you must pursue more of everything or there is something wrong with you. I wanted to fit in and be counted among the village so I looked at the banner and shouted out loud **"MORE!"**

There's nothing wrong with this banner in the square as it causes many to push on to brighter tomorrows and hope for a better future. However, I was already living my dream. I just didn't know it because every morning I got up I yelled out **"MORE!"** If I wanted to live among the village, then I had to pursue more of everything, not speak of my suicide and act like it never happened. This set my life up to break rule number three: respecting my limitations. Post-traumatic stress disorder is a normal reaction to an abnormal situation. The scars cannot be seen and most villagers don't suffer from it or it wouldn't be an abnormal situation. Like the factory worker with a burnt hand inside of the glove, I had to keep up with the other workers and ignore my burnt hand.

More is the opposite of satisfied. More can hide the treasures in front of our eyes and rush us through life and miss the things we value most. *Where satisfied may cause us to pause and value the treasures before us.* More pushes and adds more environmental stress. A healthy villager experiences stress because it comes as a normal part of life there. A villager with post-traumatic stress disorder is subject to the same stress but also has the scars from within causing stress to push outward. This core of memories can be toxic and interfere with life in the village. Like my earlier example of the worker with the burnt hand, the pain and scars from the fire's trauma interfered with his ability to work. Not being able to keep up, he is terminated and suffers a loss in his quality of life. Not being able to always keep up due to unseen scars, a person who suffers with PTSD life can suffer loss of quality of life. Perhaps, loss of employment, divorce, social isolation, suicidal ideations, and drug or alcohol abuse offset the pain left behind by the trauma.

With a new family, I quit my job as a bouncer and went back into healthcare. This would provide enough income to take care of my family. I felt fresh because I had two years to sleep to restore the core of my being. I was nervous about my past struggles, but had every confidence I'd never see a repeat of my twenties and teens. A new family meant a new house and a new house always meant **"MORE"**. A mortgage meant more hours to pay the bill. With more hours at work, leading to more responsibility and more stress. With a new home there were more bills to pay and more taxes to heap more stress on my core. The neighbors were getting more of everything. More furniture, more vacations, more cars, more education, more savings by always getting better interest rates on their homes or more additions on their homes. I wanted to be among them and every day I looked at the banner and yelled **"MORE"** because I had to keep up at the factory. I ignored my scars and burns and pushed more because my past was in the past. I couldn't totally hide. My hand hurt inside of the glove and some of the workers would complain about the way I handled my time around the factory.

Healthcare, I found, boiled off so much of the cooling water I had to make another career change or risk another meltdown, and this was out of the question. Eighteen years after I shot myself my wife and I had our first child. My wife and I thought it would be in our families' best interest if she quit work to stay at home with our daughter. We went from a two income family to one income. This shock to my system caused much of the water to drain off as my family's financial needs rested on my shoulders alone. I had struggled in health care the moment I went back to work in it. Much of my time in it reminded me of my days in school when I struggled to concentrate and multitask. I thought I would be in a better position if I made a career change.

I sold my house to get my equity and make a career change. The equity bought me some time. I didn't feel as taxed, and the core was back in the green light area. I left healthcare and went into sales work. When I started sales I found it had its own challenges as well. To be a good salesman you have to go beyond looking to the banner **"MORE"** you have to carry a placard with you everywhere you go to remind yourself to always push for **"MORE"**. The sales training manuals I read demanded I push for more. I wanted to be the best salesman ever so I pushed myself to do **"MORE"**. I wanted to be a part of the village and leave my past forever behind. "**MORE**" is not a bad thing and in order for a company to stay in business and make profit they need salesmen to always push for more. More can improve a person's quality of life and raise their children's standard of living over the one they had growing up.

This is what I sought to do. When I entered sales, twenty years had passed since my shooting. My wife and I had another child, and she was surprisingly expecting our third. I wanted **"MORE"** like the other villagers. I simply ignored my own rule to respect my limitations. The harder I pushed, the more water drained away. The more water that left; more of the rods came to the surface. The more rods meant more of the beast's ugly head started to show up. Since I could never admit to the shooting and acted like it never happened, I started to fall into a deep depression. The cycle of my teens and late twenties started to show back up.

It had been eight years since my father had thrown my things out of the house. My wife and I had our third child. Prior to this time, I only saw him once or twice a year. There were days when my family would drive past our home as they went to visit other family and never call to say they were passing through. Eight years after my father threw me out of his house, my parents got a divorce. With my father divorced and nowhere to go he showed up in my community. At first, the relationship went well. There were many changes to my life and I thought he wanted to be a part of our life. For a couple of months, it seemed he did want to be grandfather and dad at last.

When I was growing up he seemed to do, say or take whatever he wanted. He started calling my house and demand I drop what I was doing and take care of his list. The list had shown back up in my life. It was a list that forced my hand in 1986. He stared calling me names again. I had gotten comfortable in my marriage and allowed my waistline to expand. He started to make rude comments about my "gut". I asked him to not call me names, but it didn't matter. His exact words to me were *"I'm your father, will always be your father and I'll call you whatever I want to call you."* Just like in the past, the names progressed to actual physical threats of harm to me.

At first, I graciously tried to help him with his list, but if my schedule conflicted with his list then he would chide me about my unwillingness to tend to him. He told me I should be thrilled to serve my father. This started to put stress on my marriage because my wife was not familiar with the list. My father did not care if his list interfered with my family time. I should put him above my wife and children. When I was growing up, I was familiar with the way he looked at other women and how he became overly charming with them. He started to go from father in- law to overly charming with my wife. I recognized it but I shook my head and brushed it aside. He started inviting her over to his house for afternoon tea. In all of my life, I have never known the man to drink afternoon tea. She denied the offer and said she needed to take care of our son's, needs but he insisted I watch the baby. I told him my son needed to be with his mom at this point. He started yelling at me and telling me what to do with my wife and family. He screamed at me for insisting my son go with my wife. The hair on my neck stood on end.

A storm was starting to build off the coast of my life and its track took it over the reactor with its vulnerable core. I saw the way he looked at my wife. His harassing demeaning phone calls insisting I run over and take care of another list. His comments about calling me whatever he wanted to call me. He was turning my family into his footstool. He viewed me as a weak, pathetic man, and he was going to take whatever he wanted from me whenever he wanted. It wasn't enough he dragged me through the rain and made me stomp tire ruts back into the ground when it rained. It wasn't enough he never told anyone about the way he made me sit in the chair for days at a time and let the world believe my shooting was a cry for help. He was here today in my home trying to take from my little family. I still wasn't ready to believe my father would be that lost, dangerous, and ill to attempt to pursue a relationship with my wife.

The storm came ashore one afternoon when my wife and I were having lunch. She told me she had something difficult to talk to me about. She told me she felt uncomfortable with my father because she said he constantly wanted hugs, and the hugs were always too long for her comfort. I never saw my father hug her before so I knew it happened when I wasn't around. She was my wife, friend and the mother to my children. She was one of the few people in my life who had never hurt me. She had brought so much life into my lonely world, and she needed me to protect her from the one person in this world I was afraid of. I thought of my little boys and how their life brings me so much joy. How I treasure picking them up and swinging them in my arms. They are a gift from God, and I am a mere humble steward of that gift. I seek only what is in their best interest and to give my life away for their life. My father called me names, threw my things on the street when I was at my lowest point in life, stripped me of my dignity as a teenager, made me live in fear, and, now, he wanted to involve himself in the best thing that had happened to my life since I was given a second chance at life. He didn't care even about my life or what it may do to my life, my wife and my children's lives. It was time I face my personal giant and confront him.

The reactor's core took a tremendous hit as the rage started to build. I shot myself that night, I wanted to walk home and return the rifle but at the last moment my fear of his list drove me back to the tree. He was in my home twenty years after that night handing me more lists, and if I didn't get the list done, he would yell and call my home seven or eight times until I went over to take care of him. Once, I was a frightened teenager who sought the release of suicide, but I wasn't that frightened teenager anymore. I was a man who loved his family and had enough of this bully who hid behind the term *"father"*. It was going to stop that day in my driveway once and for all.

I called him on the phone and asked him to come to my home. I needed to speak with him. As I waited for him, I remembered the father who once took me fishing and bought me chocolate milk. I wish I knew where his life went so off the track and where my dad had gone and not this man who hid behind the term "father" as if that title gave him permission to take and demand from his family. He arrived at my home and approached me in the driveway. He denied all of it and said my wife was over reacting. He started to walk past me and said he would go in and straighten things out with my wife. I moved in front of him and told him this was between the two of us. He got angry with me, but my wife was safe and secure in her home and I wasn't going to allow anyone to take that from her. He demanded I let him pass and once more pulled out his credentials and waved them in front of my face insisting the term "Father" gave him full access to go anywhere in my life he wanted to go. He looked at me with pity and disgust. In his opinion, I was never going to be the man he ever was and he turned and left my home.

I was shocked by the encounter and called my step mother to get her insights. What my step-mother said to me made my grief and anger worse as I tried to wrap my head around my father's destructive demonstration towards my family. She said she wasn't surprised at all with his behavior; she was just surprised it hadn't started sooner. I was stunned no one warned me this may be a problem and she went on to tell me he had tried the same thing with my first marriage. She knew my father approached my first wife; and no one told me about it then. The words she once told me came home to roost: *"I saw you were in trouble but was afraid to say anything."* She looked the other way because she was afraid and a child's life was nearly destroyed. She looked the other way when my father made inappropriate advances towards my first wife and kept that information to herself and her concerns when he washed ashore in our little world. I thought my family would circle the wagons and help me with my father and perhaps he would get help. I never got the support from my family because our phone rang off the hook. From what the messages on the answering machine said, I was doing my "father" wrong and needed to be there for them. My fears and concerns for my family, my wife, my children were all disregarded as if it was my role to allow him to strip anything of value from my family's life because he was entitled to it. Twenty years after I nearly died from a self-inflicted gun-shot wound as a result of the fractured life I knew as a child, I had confronted my giant. I divorced myself from my family to protect a new family tree that had taken root in good soil.

A year after this confrontation and two years after making my career change the economy ground to a halt. I was the only income provider for my wife, teenage step daughter, a little girl and her two little brothers 15 months apart. The reactor's core was losing precious cooling water daily. The stress was building from the inside and outside of my life. The bills flew in faster than I could make commission. Then my family was dealt a serious blow when my father in law passed away suddenly without warning. His absence is still missed in our lives as he was a wise and loving father, husband and friend.

I had not seen the muzzle flash in ten years, but the stress was starting to cause the bullet fragment near my spine to vibrate. This was my signal the muzzle flash was not far off, and I needed to get the memory rods back under cooling water. I sold off my second house to gain access to my equity to keep food on the table and keep my past away from my family and me. I couldn't run to the caves like I had done in the past. The caves were no place to raise a family so I was going to have to try and stand my ground against the memories coming for me. By selling my house I had bought myself time and my stress level lowered. I was 39 years- old and spent my life trying to protect myself from something I'd done 22 years before. The moment was over faster than a flash of light is recorded in the brain, but there was enough energy behind that bullet to follow me decades into my future.

We moved back to the same community we lived before we sold our first home. What I didn't know about my life was, whenever my life was under stress for any period of time I started to make disruptive changes to my life to keep the core of my life at a safe temperature. Keeping this core at an acceptable level was the most important thing in my life so I could live. It was my fear of being hurt that ultimately drove me to shoot myself. My core back then hit an unsafe level, and I responded with suicide and my self-preservation mechanism was never going to allow this to happen again. The memories were so real my brain would believe I was in danger once more. I always had to keep an eye on my center which required a certain amount of energy. The more stress my environment poured on me the less time I could devote to keeping an eye on the reactor. With less energy to devote to monitoring the control panel, the memories would get more frequent and vivid. The fear of facing the muzzle flash and the beast on the other side of the veil meant I started to shut down from life. When my brain sees this it believes I am going to die so everything takes a back seat to this desire to live though I am safe. Over my life my careers suffered, my family suffered and my quality of life went down.

The slow economy followed us to our next address as well as the bills and need for groceries. The bills came in faster than I could move products and more of the reactors core fell away. I was running out of options and felt like I was being pushed into a corner. My wife was seeing changes in me. She saw things in my eyes that worried her. I knew what change she saw because the beast was starting to stir once more. I loved my family with all of my heart and I knew they didn't fully understand my past and the danger I was in from it. I was trapped because I couldn't run to the caves and get the desperately needed rest because I couldn't raise a family in the caves. I knew I couldn't keep the pressure building against the wall of the core because that meant all of the memories from the past would explode into my life. My marriage was showing signs of stress from the post-traumatic stress disorder symptoms and a friend recommended marriage counseling. It did not take very long for the counselor to ask me if my shooting bothered me. I lightly chuckled at her question as it happened over twenty years in the past and I was over it. She disagreed with me and so I started on a journey to understand what post- traumatic stress disorder was. I ignorantly imagined it was something combat veterans experienced. I never imagined my life could've been so ravaged by it all of those years later.

THE BEAST RETURNS

During my marriage counseling, I found I enjoyed writing and would share my work on different social network sites and many would encourage me to write. I started a book in the summer of 2011. It had been 26 years after my shooting and something I never talked about. My chest hurt more often, and I chalked it up as me feeling my age. My scars never bothered me like they did in my teens and twenties. I was busy being a dad and husband and settled into life. After a few months, I got bogged down in my book and put in on a shelf and took a few month off for the holidays. Business was still off from where I needed to be for my company and my personal income needs. I started to find myself overwhelmed with familiar bouts of anxiety and fears. I had not felt these tremors since I had gotten married. I would find myself wanting to curl up in a fetal position and protect my eyes from the sun. I started to see the powder blue coat again and taste the bitter flavor of gunpowder. I would snap at my family and slam cabinet doors. In the middle of the night, I'd wake to nightmares and during the day I'd feel like I was suffocating. I knew what was coming for me and it was only a matter of time before I saw the muzzle flash. I had to get the water back in the core so I sold off my remaining asset to buy time. I was able to pay some bills and buy Christmas Presents for my children.

When I sold off my truck to access its equity, I was officially done. I could no longer balance the two worlds to maintain equilibrium. I wasn't going to drag my family to the caves so that only left one other option. I would have to stand and face my past. There was no other place to go.

Shortly after selling off my truck and the first part of 2012, my wife saw an ad at the library advertising a short story contest. She knew I found writing relaxing and it may help me with my stress. She recommended I write about my story and what happened after I shot myself 26 years prior. I looked into self-publishing and thought I could bring some extra money into our home if I went that route. So I sat down and wrote "When an Angel Intervenes". I was tired of feeling depressed and used up after 26 years of living as a reanimated monster. I felt like a failure as a father and husband for having to sell off everything we ever owned to keep the lights on. The economy had been trying to bury me for years. My body ached on most days, and I was starting to feel like giving up.

I was halfway through "When an Angel Intervenes" when something happened to change my life and outlook. I was feeling depressed and worn out as was my normal mood. I was on my way to work when I walked through our living room in search of my car keys. My son was enjoying his morning routine and watching cartoons on the television. I bent down to give him a kiss goodbye when I felt a static charge ripple through my body, and this charge opened up a window to my past. This static charge was familiar because I felt it once before. When I stood up from kissing my son the ground, I stood on was also familiar.   My son could not see he and I were in **the** woods. He continued to munch on cereal and watch his cartoons unaware that he and I were no longer in our living room. I could see my warm moist breath rise into the cold winter's evening air. I gently rubbed my little boys and saw the tree I sat in front of 26 years before. I saw myself after the shooting. I saw the fear, loneliness, and suffering then I saw him reach out for hope when he said, *"I want to be a father."* I watched him struggle to his feet and start to move towards life and away from the place a lie had led him to. My son's spoon clinked against the bowl, and he giggled at his cartoons.

I wanted to know love and know the joy of fatherhood. I wanted to live more than I wanted to die. Hope had always drawn me towards life and here, twenty-six years after that day, I stood alive listening to my son munch on his cereal. Though I didn't have the opportunity to serve as a policeman and had other doors close on my life, *this door was held wide open for me and this was my true heart's desire.* I'd been given more than a second chance at life. I'd been given an abundant life, and the stress of chasing after ***more*** and trying to live my life apart from my past had made me lose sight of that. I had been spared that day and my instinct the moment I woke up was to tell the world what God had delivered me from and to warn of the lie suicide told me. I wanted to warn others to not go over the wall, to not pull back the veil because on the other side stood a dreadful beast. The violence snapped the prerecorded message found in suicides message and caused me to regret pulling the trigger. At every turn in life, I'd been apologizing for something I couldn't undo and pretend never happened. I'd felt trapped in a body society scorned because it was covered in scars from suicide. This had robbed me of the joy I'd been given. When the beast was denied taking my physical life, it sought to take my life's joy from me. It sought to destroy my life with the after-effects suicide brought with it. While trying to fit in among society I'd forgotten what really mattered, and it was in my heart and munching on cereal next to me.

When I asked God to deliver my life, He did. He not only delivered me from death that day, but He also extended eternal mercy to me. Like the thief on the cross next to Jesus granted eternal life, when I asked God to forgive me of my sin and be the Lord of my life I'd been given the joy of eternal life. I was also promised the joy through the joy that comes with having a personal relationship with Jesus Christ. He promised me in His word "the joy of the Lord is my strength," and I knew the joy of being a daddy. My life was overflowing with goodness. All I had to do was look. I yanked my son out of his chair with his spoon still in his hand and held him for dear life. I thanked God for His goodness and asked Him to restore what had been lost over the years and to put a new heart in me.

I have learned a lot about life over the last twenty-six years. One of the things I have learned is when I take a stand in my life, it's not long before it's challenged and this was no different. Writing two books on my past unlocked the gate where the beast stayed. It stepped into my life once more. This time was different and not like the last time I faced this moment in 1996.

My post-traumatic symptoms were severe but it would not prevail against me. PTSD would not own me nor steal my joy that was mine. I had mighty weapons to fight it this time, and I was ready to face this giant down once and for all. I had developed a core group of friends as I started writing this book and their support gave me incredible strength. I had the love of a supportive and compassionate wife who held my hand when the flashbacks were so severe I had to go to the hospital. I also had the peace and joy of knowing I had the God that never left my side and the battle belonged to Him. I would be able to see this storm through and the sun always comes back out.

I have started counseling. I do my own research on PTSD to better understand what it did to my life and to accept that it's a scar from what happened. My scars mean I'm alive. My marriage has grown stronger, and I've seen an outpouring of support I'd never seen before. For the first time, the beast was running away from me and not me running from it.

JOHN 10:10

"The thief only comes to steal and kill and destroy;

I have come that they may have life

And have it to the full"

John 10:10 (NIV) reveals the true nature of the thief. The thief comes to steal, kill and destroy. Depression is a disease that can be treated and suicide can be prevented. My self-inflicted gun-shot wound was a result of years of depression, and it could have been treated and avoided. As a person who suffered a near fatal suicide attempt on January 24th, 1986, when I read John 10:10 I can't ignore the description of the thief. From the first impulsive thought to after the gun went off as I read this scripture I am reminded of suicide's nature. Suicide presented itself as a friend I could trust in a time of need, but in the end it was the thief in John 10:10.

The thief promised me three things: *Peace, Release, and Escape.* At every turn in my life from the first time I heard its siren like whisper until I pulled the trigger, the thief stood in my path insisting suicide was the only way. Not only did the thief lie to me it was noticeably quiet after I pulled the trigger. It'd dogged my heels for seven months and even taunted me to pull the trigger, and once the gun went off ,it seemed to me the thief was satisfied it had delivered me into a trap. *At no time was I relieved I'd finally shot myself.* After I blew the veil back between life and death, the thief didn't come out and comfort me with these words *"Sit tight it will be over in a few minutes and soon you will be home."* In fact, my initial reaction was *"Oh God, what did I do to myself?"* None of the promises made were delivered into my life in fact what I got was: *Agony, Terror, and Remorse.* The thief never reveals their identity and hides in the shadows looking for an opportunity to steal things of value. Suicide hid its true nature from me in an attempt to steal a valued treasure.

That valued treasure was my life. I realized life was a valuable gift, and it had been given to me by God.

The text found in John 10:10 calls the thief a "killer". I was under a hypnotic trance for seven months. All of us are born with a fight or flight response mechanism to protect us from danger, and it's one of the strongest responses we have. The potent promises I'd been listening to were strong enough for me to systematically dismantle my own protection system so I wasn't fearful of shooting myself. I have memories of dying a violent death as a result of what I did to myself. Though the memories are a consequence of what I did they do serve to remind me I'm alive. It was my intent to never come out of the woods alive and carried out a plan destined to send me into the afterlife. If I'd been successful carrying out my plans I would not have these memories.

The thief also comes to destroy. This thief sought to destroy my community. There were times when the lie insisted my family, school and anyone who knew me would be better off without me. I've had the pleasure of meeting kind people while I worked on this book acquainted with the destructive after effects suicide leaves behind. Many of the people I've met were left facing an appearance of a never ending abyss when an integral part of their life vanished without so much a goodbye. The emotional destruction this causes is not realized for years, decades or perhaps a lifetime. The space of an abyss is so vast it'd take a lifetime to measure because it takes a lifetime to measure the void an absent person has created in the life of one left behind.

Though my suicide wasn't fatal it did destroy parts of my life. It destroyed my body. Prior to suicide I had a healthy body, and after the beast was finished with me, its jagged claw marks covered most of my body and it left me in physical pain. The pain can range from a dull throb to a tearing sensation through my chest wall. I no longer felt like a healthy vibrant teenager because I aged a lifetime in a day. The stigma surrounding my attempted suicide with a firearm destroyed my sense of belonging to my community. The term stigma means to bear a mark of shame. One of the biggest stigmas in our culture is mental illness. There has been no escaping my past because I bear the marks of suicide over my chest and back. I've never been able to escape my own body. For years I've never felt safe in the village when my secret got out.

Many times a person expressing a harsh, cruel, or thoughtless sentiments only expressed them from a personal issue from their past. Their hurt, anger, or ignorance formed from a prior experience with suicide gave them a chance to sound off at me for another person's suicide.

I started the story of my life telling the story of another man's life. The blind man was wandering around in an oppressive darkness without sight. I was living under an oppressive darkness as suicide led me into a patch of isolated woods to shoot myself in the chest. The blind man didn't know or have a relationship with the Master like many of the crowds following Jesus at the time. I wasn't a Christian, rarely stepped foot in a church and never read my King James New Testament pocket-sized bible that I went with me into the woods. One seemingly random day, an obscure blind man met God in flesh. A single touch gave sight to this man and radically changed his life. One random day on a calendar, I chose to remove my life from this world from the pull of a trigger. I offered up a simple heart felt prayer to God, Himself. A single touch restored my life following that pull on the trigger.

The only reason why I knew to call out to God came from faithful servants of God that felt compelled to share of the goodness of God. These servants told me God sent His son Jesus to die on a cross so I could have everlasting life. They shared with me John 3:16-17 (NIV):

> *"For God so loved the world that he gave his only Son, that whoever believes in him shall not perish but have eternal life. For God did not send His son into the world to condemn the world, but to save the world through Him."*

These people God placed along my life told me God loved me like a father and wanted a relationship with me. In His word, He promised in Jeremiah 29:11:

> *"For I know the plans I have for you, declares the Lord, plans to prosper you and not to harm you, plans to give you hope and a future."*

In Matthew 11:28-29:

> *"Come to me, all you who are weary and burdened, and I will give you rest. Take my yoke upon you and learn from me, for I am*

gentle and humble in heart, and you will

find rest for your hearts."

The thief told me there was no hope for my future and I'd be better off dead. The thief promised me for many months I'd know peace, but when it came time to pull the trigger I hesitated for a moment. It then started to taunt and scream at me **"Pull the trigger!"** After I pulled the trigger and the thief left me alone to die, the comforting peace that followed me through that drama came from only one source. It was not from the thief and it was nothing I did. It came from the one whom made the promise in Matthew 11:28-29.

In John 10:10, it says that thief is a killer and a destroyer but God came that we may have life. The thief sought to kill and destroy my life, but God says in His word

"He has come so that they may have life."

In Colossians 1:15 (NIV) it says:

"He is the invisible God, the firstborn over

all of creation."

In Philippians 2 5-8(NIV):

"In your relationships with one another,

having the same mindset as Christ Jesus:

Who, being in very nature God, did not

*consider equality with God something to be
used to His own advantage; rather, he made
himself nothing by taking the very nature of
a servant, being made in human likeness.
And being found in appearance as a man,
he humbled himself by becoming obedient
to death-even on a cross."*

I found though the thief sought to destroy my life, God came in the form of man known as Jesus Christ so that I may have life. The thief never delivered any of the promises it made. I earnestly sought God from the pit of despair asking Him to deliver my life from that moment, twenty five years have passed since that prayer, and I am alive today.

Though the thief left me to die alone, I lived with the close presence of Jesus Christ when I went into the valley of the shadow of death. Romans 8:37-39 (NIV) Christ declares:

*"No, in all these things we are more than
conquerors through him who loved us. For I
am convinced that neither death nor life,
neither angels nor demons, neither the
present nor the future, nor any powers,*

neither height nor depth, nor anything else

in all creation, will be able to separate us

from the love of God that is in Christ Jesus".

The lie told me I was alone and all was lost but as I went into the trauma room that night I found that to be untrue. God demonstrated His faithful love to me by making good on His promises. He never let go of me once I called out to Him.

Not only does John 10:10 (NIV) declare, *"I have come that they may have life"* it goes on to make an additional promise *"And have it to the full."* At my lowest point in life God showed me I could not only live but have a full life. While the thief was busy trying to take and destroy my life God was offering me a life and a full life at that. There is not a day that does not go by that I do not rejoice when I hear small voices tell me "Daddy, I love you" or one of my personal favorites "You're the best daddy!" Where I knew death Christ gave me life. He became my friend when I was in the pit of despair. He restored my life and set a table for me and asked me to go and share the good news there is life in Him.

I knew when I woke up in the hospital; I'd been given an incredible gift. A second chance at life should never be taken for granted. I understand we take for granted what we have until we lose something. We take good health for granted until we are sick. I took my life for granted until the moment I thought it had been lost. I wanted to honor this gift since the first day of my second chance at life. I wanted to be a good steward with this gift and by God's goodness, He has provided me with a future to bless me with this heart's desire to share the same Hope I found. My heart has always been heavy for those who succumb to suicide. My fear has always been how many have the same moment of regret?

"When an Angel Intervenes" started this chapter in my life. Had it never been for that book or my pen name "Christian Price" I never would have opened up about my life or attempted to share what I learned about suicide. It was when I finished this book did I realize I owe myself something silver. I wanted something of silver to celebrate my 25th anniversary of life. To commemorate and celebrate my 25 years of life, I started an outreach to help those who are in that struggle.

The name of my outreach is called the *"The Christian Price Suicide to Life Project: Fighting the Lie of*

Suicide with Truth and Hope." The mission statement of the project is found in Luke 4:18(NIV):

> *"The spirit of the Lord is on me, because He has anointed me to proclaim good news to the poor. He has sent me to proclaim freedom for the prisoners and recovery of sight for the blind to set the oppressed free."*

This is the hope of the project: Shed light on suicide in hopes some will see it for what it is, a lie and thief. Once some see it for what it is then my hope is they will move away from it and back towards life. Once they have taken steps back towards life my further hope is they will continue on to know an abundant and satisfied life.

I've found five keys during my life that enabled me to move from suicide and back towards life. The first two keys have the highest priority because these are the only two keys that are inside of my heart. These two keys don't rely on other people or my circumstances. Life is never static, and can change without a moment's notice. People will fail us and sometimes they are the ones we love and trust the most in life. At times these were the only two keys I possessed, but they kept me alive and standing firm against the lie testing my resolve to see the next day.

The first key is the master key to my life and this involved asking Jesus Christ into my life. The night when I went out to "end it all", I prayed to God asking Him to deliver my life. I really didn't want to die but I was committed enough to my goal of ending my despair. The actual killing was nothing more than a temporary hindrance towards reaching the goal. Then the gun went off and the truth of the moment woke me up to a new reality and nothing could've prepared me for it. Less than two weeks after pulling the trigger, God sent a messenger to accept his plan of salvation for my life. She told me one of God's desires for my life was to have a relationship with me. She pointed out scriptures that described a friend like relationship with Him, John 15:13 (NIV):

> *"Greater love has no one than this: to lay down one's life for one's friends."*

In scripture, Jesus laid his life down willingly, John 10:17-18 (NIV):

> *"The reason my Father loves me is that I lay down my life —only to take it up again.* [18] *No one takes it from me, but I lay it down of*

my own accord. I have authority to lay it
down and authority to take it up again. This
command I received from my Father."

God describes love as sacrificial by laying down one's life for the good of a friend. Jesus says he willingly lays down his life for us but how do we know God considers us a friend? John 15: 14 (NIV):

"You are my friends if you do what I
command"

Then, what is the greatest command I wondered? Matthew 22: 37-38 (NIV): Jesus replied:

"Love the Lord your God with all your heart
and with all your soul and with all your
mind.'(38) This is the first and greatest
commandment"

I knew a relationship was a two- way street. When I asked God into my heart and be at the center of my life he became close like a friend. She shared with me scripture of how God viewed me in my new found relationship, John 15: 15 (NIV):

"I no longer call you servants, because a
servant does not know his master's
business. Instead, I have called you friends,

for everything that I learned from my Father
I have made known to you."

Like any close relationship there were benefits and a relationship, with God was no different. I could know what God's purpose and plan were for my life based on this scripture. The bible told me nothing could separate me from the love of God: Romans 8:38-39 (NIV):

"For I am convinced that neither death nor
life, neither angels nor demons, neither the
present nor the future, nor any powers,(39)
neither height nor depth, nor anything else
in all creation, will be able to separate us
from the love of God that is in Christ Jesus
our Lord."

The bible also told me God never sleeps, Psalm 121:4(NIV):

"Indeed, he who watches over Israel will
neither slumber nor sleep."

God had demonstrated to me above all He was trustworthy of my life in His care. She showed me God had a plan and purpose for my life in Jeremiah 29:11 (NIV):

"For I know the plans I have for you,"
declares the LORD, "plans to prosper you

and not to harm you, plans to give you hope

and a future."

Further study showed me in Romans 8:28 (NIV)

"And we know that in all things God works

for the good of those who love him, who

have been called according to his purpose".

Hope and truth are mighty weapons against suicidal thoughts. With the hope and truth found in Jesus Christ, this life giving relationship makes this the first of the five keys.

The second key I found to move away from suicide and back towards life was the vow to protect my life. Genesis 1:27 (NIV):

"So God created man in his own image, in

the image of God he created him; male and

female he created them."

Since scripture told me I was made in the image of God my life was a gift from Him. As I was losing my life I hated I had quit on "me". I became aware of another person and it wasn't the skin and bone sack I knew as "me". 2 Corinthians 5:1 (NIV)

"Now we know that if the earthly tent we

live in is destroyed, we have a building from

God, an eternal house in heaven, not built

by human hands."

My spirit was grieved the tent I believed to be myself had been used as a weapon against the real "me". This added to my emotional despair as a result of suicide. I made a vow to myself to never again use my tent as a weapon against the real me. I vowed to never take my life again.

As I walked life's road I never knew I discovered five keys that saved, sustained and transformed my life from January 24, 1986 until I wrote this book. As I looked at history, it occurred to me the strength of the first two keys was found in relation to where they were located at in my life. Keys one and two were inside of my heart and my environmental circumstances couldn't touch those keys. John 7:38 (NIV):

"Whoever believes in me, as Scripture has

said, rivers of living water will flow from

within them."

I found no one can force me to break my vow; only I make that choice to keep or break it. Numbers 30:2 (NIV):

"When a man makes a vow to the Lord or

takes an oath to obligate himself by a

> pledge, he must not break his word but
> must do everything he said."

I also found by having the first key in my life there was strength but it wasn't my own strength, 1John 4:4 (NIV):

> "You, dear children, are from God and have
> overcome them, because the one who is in
> you is greater than the one who is in the
> world."

Suicide thrived in a lie that told me I couldn't go on anymore. My vow to protect my life was tested when I was living in my car for a season. It seemed like I couldn't go on another day, but the truth reminded me I was enjoying a one dollar cup of coffee. I wanted another day to have more coffee. I could go on and resist the lie of suicide.

The next three keys focus on my environment. The third key I noticed was the need for a supportive environment or a buddy system. My suicidal past was most tested when I was alone. Genesis 2:18 (NIV):

> "The Lord God said, "It is not good for the
> man to be alone. I will make a helper
> suitable for him."

We were not meant to be alone and I found I was at my lowest points in life when I was alone. A buddy system is a powerful ally when fighting suicides addictive promises of release. I found I wasn't born with a desire to shoot myself. My shooting was a symptom of a much deeper problem. When a person possesses the third key, qualified mental health professionals should be consulted to address why suicide seems like an attractive offer. It's been my experience with the beast, it rarely shows up during office hours. This is when national suicide crisis hotlines are valuable should a crisis erupt. One of the reasons why I chose to shoot myself was the years of verbal abuse. In order to move from suicide to life, destructive relationships need to be addressed. Proverbs 18:21 (NIV):

> *"The tongue has the power of life and death, and those who love it will eat its fruit."*

In my despair I believed I had no more value than an animal. This lack of self-worth made me believe the world would be a better place without me. These were lies and not the truth. By having the first key God and His word at the center of our life this key defeats the lies suicide uses against our life. He is the ultimate "buddy system" to have in life to move from suicide and back towards life. Psalm 91: 9-11 (NIV):

> *"If you say 'The Lord is my refuge', and you make the Most High you dwelling, (10) no harm will overtake you, no disaster will come near your tend. (11)For he will command his angels concerning you to guard you in all your ways."*

The beast of suicide and its lingering legacy couldn't overcome my life with God at the center. I found suicide's lies to be powerful and seductive as it sought to ruin me, but God's truth states in Isaiah 54:17 (NIV):

> *"No weapon forged against you will prevail, and you will refute every tongue that accuses you. This is the heritage of the servants of the Lord, and this is their vindication from me, declares the Lord."*

When the lie of suicide says "there's no hope, your family is better off without you, you have no purpose", there in Isaiah 54:17 is a signed written statement from God himself. These lies will not prevail against the one who has God in their life because He is the master key to all five keys. If there are destructive chemical dependencies they need to be addressed. I've never had my life ravaged by a drug addiction so I'm unable to speak to it. I do know anyone who struggles under these addictions are at high risk to suicide. Key 3 is to grab hold of addiction oriented therapy either counselors or support groups.

The fourth key is based on living life as if you've been given a second chance to live. It's our nature to take things for granted until they are no longer with us. On the day I shot myself, I assumed it was going to be my last day and I found I didn't want to miss out on a single thing or the things I'd taken for granted over the years. I never knew how much joy I would find in seeing a bird or a tree. I never knew how much I wanted to taste ice cream once more. I didn't know I had a bucket list hidden within me, and deep down, I wanted to grow up one day and be a dad. Suicide's lies had stolen my life, but I was given a reprieve and another chance to live. There isn't a more powerful moment in my life than when I woke up in the Intensive Care Unit and knew I'd been given the chance to live again. If you've lived under the burden of suicidal thoughts, previous attempts or have lived under a cloud of despair and have grasped the Christian Price Suicide to Life

Project, I want you to live from this moment forward with the attitude of being given the same gift I was given. You may not have recovered in an ICU from a near- fatal moment, but it doesn't mean suicide isn't already stealing from your life. Mark this day with a personal memento and carry it with you. Use pictures, necklaces, tattoos, but mark the date as this being the rest of your life. My never again date was January 24, 1986, and my reminders have always been my scars.

With the 4th key secured in your heart it's time to live your life to the fullest measure. If you have ever wanted to finish college go do it. If you wanted to learn how to fly an airplane this is the moment you've always wanted. Since you were given the second chance to live your life don't squander the gift. Let no opportunity slip past you. Make amends when you can and shake the dust off your feet from the toxic relationships and move on when you can't. John 10:10 (NIV):

> *"The thief comes only to steal and kill and destroy; I have come that they may have life, and have it to the full."*

Suicide is the thief that has come to steal, kill and destroy but Christ has come so we may live and live life to the fullest measure. If you possess the first key in your heart Christ will not only deliver your life from the snare of suicide, but He will see your life is full. There will be hope, purpose, peace, and life. It doesn't mean easy- street shows up. It means God dwells in your heart, and He will calm the storm inside of you or calm the storms outside of you.

The fifth key of this project takes your personal gifts and invest them into another life. I found suicide attacked my self-esteem and sense of value. I believed I wouldn't be missed and I had nothing I could offer to society. This is the key I'm currently working on. By possessing this key I've found I've lived beyond suicide. Helping other lives based on my personal struggle with suicide has been a very enriching experience for my life, and it has brought about remarkable healing to it. Psalm 139:14 (NIV):

> *"I praise you because I am fearfully and wonderfully made; your works are wonderful, I know that full well."*

God considers us a wonderful creation made in His image. God put talents and abilities inside of us for us to use to serve Him and others. 1st Peter 4:10 (NIV):

> *"Each of you should use whatever gift you have received to serve others, as faithful stewards of God's grace in its various forms."*

Or Galatians 5:13-14 (NIV):

> *"For you were called to freedom, brothers. Only do not use your freedom as an opportunity for the flesh, but through love serve on another. For the whole law is fulfilled in one word: 'You shall love your neighbor as yourself.'"*

Another verse Mark 10:45 (NIV):

> *"For even the Son of Man did not come to be served, but to serve, and to give his life as a ransom for many."*

Many times the best medicine is focusing outward and serving others. Take a moment and take inventory of your life and find what you believe to be a gift or gifts. Do you have your own struggles you have overcome that you could share and offer advice to be a blessed hope to another life? If so, share your experiences. Volunteer at the hospital, nursing home, some communities have volunteer fire and ambulance needs. Perhaps you attend a place of worship and they have needs. Maybe you see a need in your community and take the bull by the horns and start an outreach of your own. However, I will caution it's important, based on my experience; the keys are permitted to unlock the other keys. It's no good to move on to the fifth key if you don't have a strong foundation with key three. It takes time to see changes. The first key is only a prayer away. If you'd like to have this key in your life now would be a great time for you to accept it into your life if you haven't already. 2 Corinthians 6:2 (NIV):

> *"For he says, In the time of my favor I heard you, and in the day of salvation I helped you. I tell you now is the time of God's favor, now is the day of salvation."*

I wouldn't have survived that shooting and all of the obstacles it posed to my life had it not been for the presence of Jesus Christ in my life. This is why "The Christian Price Suicide to Life Project" has placed Him as the first key. Just as my friend in 1986 shared with me God's plan of salvation, I'd like to share that with you. Revelation 3:20 (NIV):

> *"Behold, I stand at the door and knock. If anyone hears my voice, and opens the door,*

I will come in to him and eat with him, and

he with me."

This scripture says its God's desire to have a relationship with us. Typically, when I open the door to someone to come inside of my house and eat with me, they were invited over. A person who sits with me in my home for a meal shares a relationship with me. If you hear Him knocking at your door, I encourage you to invite Him in and not deny yourself of His life transforming power.

We are separated from a relationship with God due to our sin nature. God is a Holy God and can't permit sin into His presence, and it's impossible for us to save ourselves from our own nature. Romans 3: 23 (NIV):

"For all have sinned and fall short of the glory of God." Ephesians 2:8-9 *" For it is by grace you have been saved, through faith- and this is not from yourselves, it is the gift of God- not by works, so that no one can boast."*

John 3:16 (NIV):

"For God so loved the world that He gave His one and only Son, that whoever believes

> in Him shall not perish but have eternal
> life."

Titus 3:5 (NIV):

> "He saved us, not because of righteous
> things we had done, but because of His
> mercy. He saved us through the washing of
> rebirth and renewal by the Holy spirit."

Our sin problem can only be addressed through God's free gift and not of ourselves.

Once we recognize we are unable to save ourselves from our own sin nature and God has provided the only solution to this problem, it's time for action. We must repent of our sinful and rebellious nature towards God. Luke 13:3 (NIV):

> "I tell you, no! But, unless you repent, you
> too will all perish."

Once you have repented of your sin, it's time to ask Christ to save you. Romans 10:13 (NIV):

> "Everyone who calls on the name of the
> Lord will be saved."

In Acts 16:31 (NIV):

> "They replied, Believe in the lord Jesus, and
> you will be saved- you and your household."

He says He will come into your life if you open the door to your life. The key is faith. Jesus replied to the thief who was dying next to Him in Luke 23:43 (NIV):

> *"Jesus answered him, Truly I tell you today you will be with me in paradise."*

Another scripture, Romans 10: 9-10 (NIV):

> *"If you declare with your mouth 'Jesus is Lord,' and believe in your heart that God raised Him from the dead, you will be saved. For it is with your heart that you believe and are justified, and with your mouth that you profess your faith and are saved."*

I know where I was on January 24, 1986. I had every intention of killing myself with that rifle. At the last possible moment, my will to live grasped a parachute because it had paid attention to people when they shared with me the Good News of God's love and plan of salvation for my life. I made one simple prayer and earnestly believed He would answer me. There was no complicated religious ceremony. Just a lonely, lost, broken- hearted teenager with a rifle and a Bible who thought he was alone in the woods that night. I prayed a simple prayer and here I am over twenty-five years later sharing with you my testimony and what God delivered my life from.

If you hear Him knocking on the door to your life and are ready to open the door, I ask you to take a moment and bow your head and ask him to come into your life by saying this prayer *"Dear Lord Jesus, I admit I am a sinner and I am in need of You and Your forgiveness. I want to turn from my sins and follow You completely. I believe You are the Son of God who died on the cross for me and all of my sins; You were buried, rose to life again and You are coming back. I accept the Father's gift of eternal life through faith and belief in You alone. I receive You as Lord and Savior of every part and area of my life forever and ever. Now Lord, fill me with Your Holy Spirit. In Jesus' name, Amen.*

If you have made this commitment to Jesus Christ by asking Him into your life I'd love to hear from you. He says in His word in Hebrews 13:5 He will never leave or forsake you. When God makes a promise, you can trust it. If you have made this commitment I urge to seek out a Christ centered church that teaches from God's love letter to you or His Holy Bible. Remember, even though He meets you where you're at, He won't leave you there. He surely didn't leave me where we met. It will be a life-transforming experience, and if He transformed my life, He will do the same for you. I will keep my contact information updated always on the cover page to this book.

May God Keep you and bless you, Jim Atkisson

Made in the USA
Charleston, SC
23 August 2013